# THE ENVIRONMENTALIST:
## ENVIRONMENTAL LAW AND POLICY

# THE ENVIRONMENTALIST:
## ENVIRONMENTAL LAW AND POLICY

**DOUGLAS JAMES JOYCE**

**Nova Science Publishers, Inc.**
*Commack, New York*

**Editorial Production:** Susan Boriotti
**Office Manager:** Annette Hellinger
**Graphics:** Frank Grucci and John T'Lustachowski
**Information Editor:** Tatiana Shohov
**Book Production:** Donna Dennis, Patrick Davin, Christine Mathosian
and Tammy Sauter
**Circulation:** Maryanne Schmidt
**Marketing/Sales:** Cathy DeGregory

*Library of Congress Cataloging-in-Publication Data*

Joyce, Douglas James
       The environmentalist: environmental law and policy / Douglas James Joyce.
               p.       cm.
       Includes bibliographic references and index.
       ISBN 1-56072-637-7
       1. Environmental policy. 2. Environmental law. 3. Environmental policy --
Colorado. 4. Environmental law -- Colorado. I. Title.
GE170.J69                 1998                                           98-51005
363.7'05—dc21                                                            CIP

Copyright © 1999 by  Nova Science Publishers, Inc.
            6080 Jericho Turnpike, Suite 207
            Commack, New York 11725
            Tele. 516-499-3103        Fax 516-499-3146
            e-mail: Novascience@earthlink.net
            e-mail: Novascil@aol.com
            Web Site: http://www.nexusworld.com/nova

The authors and publisher have taken care in preparation of this book, but make no
expressed or implied warranty of any kind and assume no responsibility for any errors or
omissions. No liability is assumed for incidental or consequential damages in connection
with or arising out of information contained in this book.

This publication is designed to provide accurate and authoritative information with regard
to the subject matter covered herein. It is sold with the clear understanding that the
publisher is not engaged in rendering legal or any other professional services. If legal or
any other expert assistance is required, the services of a competent person should be
sought. FROM A DECLARATION OF PARTICIPANTS JOINTLY ADOPTED BY A
COMMITTEE OF THE AMERICAN BAR ASSOCIATION AND A COMMITTEE OF
PUBLISHERS.

*Printed in the United States of America*

To Pamela Shaw Joyce --
   who makes the world beautiful
   wherever we go.

*Those who would govern wisely*
*Must first respect life.*

Lao Tzu
from *Tao Teh Ching*

# CONTENTS

# PREFACE

The preservationist sees natural wonders and wants to hold them unblemished for all time. The conservationist sees natural resources and wants to ensure their viability for future generations. The ecologist sees the relationships between species and the world they inhabit, and wants to maintain a healthy ecosystem.

The environmentalist sees all of these as one and the same.

Many words have been used to describe those who would protect the environment. John Muir, who in the 19th Century led the crusade for the creation of Yosemite National Park and other wilderness sanctuaries, was a preservationist. Gifford Pinchot, founder of the scientific forest management practices used by the U.S. Forest Service throughout the 20th Century, was a conservationist. Aldo Leopold, who often referred to himself as a conservationist, is now regarded as an ecologist.

So who is an environmentalist? More importantly, are you?

# INTRODUCTION

As I put together these essays, I realize they depict my own personal evolution as an environmentalist. In the course of writing them, I became aware of profound problems in the current discourse on environmental law and policy. I found that most authors are unaware of their own relationship with the planet. They talk as if the environment is something outside of them. Their observations are completely anthropocentric, that is, they regard welfare of the human species as the sole reason for existence. Their environmentalism is limited to that which is good for people. This results in a sense of separation from the environment that is more than unrealistic – it is unhealthy, for people as well as the planet. When they make environmental law and policy, they further remove themselves from reality by separating themselves from the policy itself. Critical thinking on issues of environmental law and policy taught me that we, the planet, and our policies are one. More than inseparable, they are unity.

## CRITICAL THINKING

*Critical thinking is one of several ways we use our minds to understand established ideas, create new ideas, or solve the never-ending flow of problems that confront us. We use* ritual thinking *when we brush our teeth every day, seemingly on autopilot. We use* random thinking *while idly looking out the window or taking a stroll without really concentrating on anything in particular. We use* appreciative thinking *when we enjoy, admire, or otherwise value our perceptions, be they of nature, of music, or of art. These are all important to our daily lives. But we use* critical thinking *when we consciously utilize our intelligence to solve problems and make decisions (Organ 1965, xii).*

Critical thinking allows us to solve problems by exploring possible answers, then testing them. The scientific method is rigorous application of critical thinking in which possible answers, known as hypotheses, are tested by experimental method and either upheld or falsified. This does not mean, however, that we must set up a physical experiment for every idea we dream up. Our imaginations are well adapted to running mental experiments that explore possible answers and test their validity against reality. We continually identify problems, postulate casual hypotheses, and test them against the world as we know it. With discipline, we expand the world as we know it through increased knowledge against which we can test our hypotheses. We also learn to accept falsified hypotheses as false – to do otherwise results in unfounded bias or prejudice. Evolutionary success is largely a matter of realizing false hypotheses and avoiding them.

Disciplined critical thinking is exercised through reading and writing. In reading, we acquire a way of seeing that is reflective and critical (Tinberg 1993, 95). We constantly test the writer's hypotheses against our own reality at the very same time that we set ourselves in the writer's world. When we turn around and write, we are able to see the structure of our thought, and open our thought processes to questioning and revision. In writing, we are forced to undergo data gathering, theory building, theory testing, and data generating processes in order to produce something that makes sense to ourselves and to other readers. It has been said that, "Writing puts students at the center of their own learning" (Clarke and Biddle 1993, pp 15-16). I encourage you to have fun with the writing exercises at the end of each essay.

## ENVIRONMENTAL LAW AND POLICY

Issues of environmental law and policy lend themselves easily to disciplined critical thinking. There are a multitude of issues, each with multiple possible answers, many of them conflicting. The issues covered in these essays run the gamut from water resources to particulate pollution in the atmosphere, from environmental economics to social ecology, but no attempt is made to exhaust the list of possible issues. There is no mention of solid municipal waste, and very little discussion of endangered species, though I consider both of these issues to lso be of paramount importance. I chose to include essays that were instrumental in my own critical thinking process. The writing of these essays led me to conclude that nearly all that I was reading was shallow policy based on anthropocentric foundations that keep the author from realizing his or her true relationship to environmental law and policy.

## WHY CRITICAL THINKING IS IMPORTANT TO THE ENVIRONMENTALIST

Critical thinking is essential to the environmentalist in order to distinguish between bias and reason, fact and opinion. It enables the environmentalist to recognize deceptive arguments as well as provable statements. The exercises at the end of each essay are designed to help you reach your own conclusions on issues of environmental law and policy, mostly through the application of writing your own versions of the essays. There are many possible answers to any given problem – the environmentalist must discover them all for the sake of the planet.

## CONCLUSION

Through writing these essays I am now able to discern my own state of personal evolution as an environmentalist. Disciplined use of critical thinking skills has shaped my perspective on environmental matters such that I find myself more accepting of information that immediately shows itself to be well founded, rather than sensational or alarmist. More than that, my entire philosophy has been altered – I now have a much better sense of my place in the world as an environmentalist. We are all environmentalists, whether we choose to consciously view ourselves that way or not. We cannot separate ourselves from the environment – to do so would mean certain death.

Similarly, we cannot separate ourselves from our environmental laws and policies. They are us. And we cannot separate the environment from environmental law and policy. They are one. We, the planet, and our policies are one. They are unity. This is what is meant by *deep policy*, the conclusion of the final essay in this book. In describing the philosophy of environmental

ethics known as deep ecology, Bill Devall and George Sessions talk about
"the work of cultivating ecological consciousness" (Devall and Sessions 1985,
8). They contrast deep ecology with "the dominant worldview of technocratic
industrial societies which regards humans as isolated and fundamentally
separate from the rest of Nature, as superior to, and in charge of, the rest of
creation" (65). *Deep policy* is about the work of cultivating consciousness.

I hope you get as much out of reading it as I got out of writing it.

## REFERENCES

Clarke, J. H., and Biddle, A. W., eds., 1993. *Teaching Critical Thinking:
Reports from Across the Curriculum.* Englewood Cliffs, NJ: Prentice-Hall,
Inc.

Devall, B., and Sessions, G. 1985. *Deep Ecology: Living as if Nature
Mattered.* Salt Lake City, UT: Peregrine Smith Books.

Organ, T. W., 1965. *The Art of Critical Thinking.* Boston, MA: Houghton
Mifflin Co.

Tinberg, H., 1993. "'Deep Play': Reading Culture in the Writing
Classroom." Clarke, J. H., and Biddle, A. W., eds., 1993. *Teaching Critical
Thinking: Reports from Across the Curriculum.* Englewood Cliffs, NJ:
Prentice-Hall, Inc.

# A DRIVE FROM DENVER TO MT. EVANS

*The environmentalist sees the impact of man as well as the beauty of nature.*
*This essay describes the changes man has wrought in the Rocky Mountains west*
*of Denver, Colorado. Aldo Leopold has the last word.*

Driving the 50 miles from City Hall in Denver, Colorado (elevation: 5280
feet) west and south to Mt. Evans (elevation: 14,264 feet) is a journey through
numerous ecosystems and microclimates. Such a drive covers about every
topographical feature known to man, and every mile of that drive is influenced
by the handiwork of man, as indeed it must be: we are taking a drive.

We head west on Colfax, once known as Electric Avenue, and immediately
cross the South Platte River. Dammed and channeled, this former high plains
riparian ecosystem is now dwarfed by the parallel concrete causeways of
Interstate 25 and railroad yards. It is the lowest point in elevation that we will
traverse, but not the lowest point in man's mistreatment of the environment.

Now climbing out of the river basin, we pass through the City of Lakewood.
Where buffalo grass and blue grama once thrived in this semi-desert grassland,
we now see nothing but exotics: oaks and roses and golf courses; planted amid
our favorite groundcovers: asphalt and concrete. In Golden, we merge with
traffic on I-70, part of our greatest national defense project, the Interstate system
of high-speed roadways.

We climb rapidly now, noticing the tremendous geologic upheavals that
formed the mountains we are entering, evidenced in stratifications in rock turned
at nearly right-hand angles to the road in the cuts made into the foothills of the
Rocky Mountains. Shrublands give way to forest as we climb swiftly passed
belching diesel trucks and motor homes, ourselves passed as though standing still
by the drivers of sedans, on their way home to Genesee and Evergreen, or

dashing up the hill to spend the day at one of the many clearcuts known as ski resorts. Stands of ponderosa pine occupy the sunny, dry mountain slopes, with their understory of grasses, shrubs, and wildflowers.

As we climb through 8,500 feet we see lodgepole pine forest on our left, the north-facing slopes. We cannot tell for sure at 65 miles per hour, but these forests have been artificially "saved" from forest fire for decades now, and are desperately in need of a burn. This successional stand has apparently been designated a climax forest by the local homeowners. There are also patches of quaking aspen, revered in this region because they are among the few species that offer autumnal coloration for beautiful October drives along the I-70 corridor.

Passing through Idaho Springs, we see the remains of Colorado's mining boom, all left to rust and rot and leach in the name of profit. We turn south toward Mt. Evans, now following, now crossing mountain riparian ecosystems dominated by alder, cottonwood, willow, and birch. As we pass through the Mount Goliath Natural Area, we see a stand of bristlecone and limber pine on rocky ground where the climate is dry and sunny with high runoff. Tree islands of fragmented Englemann spruce and subalpine fir are now visible. Were we to stop the car, we would see the forest floor there littered with rotting logs and abundant tree seedlings. Life is slow at these elevations -- slow to grow and slow to decay, but our vehicle, though noticeably affected by the altitude, still carries us swiftly up the Highest Road in the U.S., as it is clearly marked in red on our Rand McNally.

We pass quickly out of the forest and into the tundra. Our very presence on this road means it must be summer, and we are treated to a multitude of wildflowers out the window. We may see mule deer and elk, and if we are especially lucky, we may see the famous mountain goats of Mt. Evans. A century ago we would have seen bighorn sheep on these slopes.

We arrive at the top, and find ourselves in a parking lot, surrounded by vehicles and tourists. We hop out to enjoy the view and the sunshine, only to immediately realize we should have brought our jackets. "Quick! Back into the car!" And in the rearview mirror, sits ecologist and conservationist, Aldo Leopold, by himself on a rock, writing:

*Thus always does history, whether of [mountain] or market place, end in paradox. The ultimate value in these [mountains] is wildness, and the [bighorn sheep] is wildness incarnate. But all conservation of wildness is self-defeating, for to cherish we must see and fondle, and when enough have seen and fondled, there is no wilderness left to cherish.* (Leopold 1949, 101)

## CRITICAL THINKING DRILLS

1.  Take an imaginary trip in your own region and describe it from the environmentalist's point of view. Are there any known environmental hazards along the way? Is the problem getting better or worse? Are there any environmental success stories that you can point to?

2.  What form of transportation are you using in your imaginary trip? How does the method of transportation affect the environment in which you are travelling? How does your own presence affect the environment that you are describing?

3.  Critique Aldo Leopold's statement regarding conservation at the end of the essay. Do you agree that "all conservation of wildness is self-defeating?" Explain your answer.

## RESEARCH FOR THE ADVENTUROUS

Read "Marshland Elegy" and "Thinking Like a Mountain," two of Aldo Leopold's essays in *A Sand County Almanac*. Write a 600-word essay comparing and contrasting these two chapters from Leopold's life as a conservationist. Describe how he grew in his chosen field and how he learned from his own mistakes.

## ACKNOWLEDGEMENT

Leopold, A. 1949. *A Sand County Almanac.* New York: Oxford University Press.

# QUESTIONING WATER RIGHTS

## AN ETHICAL ANALYSIS OF THE CITY OF AURORA'S SOUTH PARK CONJUNCTIVE USE PROJECT

*The environmentalist must often use tools other than economic analysis to decide the appropriateness of human actions. In this essay, ethical analysis is used to find a project to divert water 80 miles from its source to a city on the eastern plains of Colorado ethically unsound. This conclusion is reached by first relating Colorado water law to our notion of property rights and utilitarianism, then exploring the questions of risk and sustainable development, before finally applying the tools of social ecology to the problem of domination of one community over another in appropriating scarce water supplies in the Colorado Rocky Mountains.*

## INTRODUCTION

South Park, 70 miles south and west of Denver, Colorado, is one of several intermountain parks located in the Colorado Rocky Mountains. As such, it is a high valley surrounded by majestic peaks, including several "fourteeners" of the Continental Divide to the west and north, and the lushly forested lesser peaks of the Kenosha Range to the east. South Park is windswept and treeless, as it lies in the rainshadow of the Divide, but through its grassy plains course the beginnings of the South Platte River and Tarryall Creek, the Platte's first major tributary. It is home to herds of antelope, elk and deer, but has long been ranched, and is the birthplace of thousands of head of cattle each year. There are few full time residents, but South Park's proximity to both the Denver and Colorado Springs metropolitan areas makes it very attractive as a weekend get-away spot.

Relatively dry though it is, South Park is no stranger to metropolitan water projects. Antero Reservoir, Spinney Mountain Reservoir, and Elevenmile Canyon Reservoir all store mountain runoff for the residents of the City and County of Denver, before it is carried away by the South Platte, a formerly quixotic stream, now tamed by the Denver Water Board.

The City of Aurora, Colorado, is looking thirstily toward South Park for answers to its future water shortages. Aurora has begun work on its South Park Conjunctive Use Project, promoted as safe and environmentally friendly. The City claims the local property owners will not be adversely affected by the project, though conjunctive use technology is untried in the area. Furthermore, Aurora is promoting the project as environmentally enhancing to South Park, as part of the design includes the introduction of wetlands where little or nothing in the way of wetlands currently exist.

This essay questions the project on two levels: 1) It questions the use of an untested technology that may adversely affect the local water supply, which is wholly dependent on groundwater. And 2) it questions the utilitarian water policies that lead to such projects, employing the tools of ethical analysis to view the project from the perspectives of sustainability, including appropriate technology and social ecology, and their affects on the communities of both South Park *and* the City of Aurora, in the present and in the future.

## BACKGROUND

As will be shown, the South Park Conjunctive Use Project has everything to do with Colorado water law. A brief discussion of Colorado water law, therefore, is required in order to set the stage for the project currently under way.

Colorado is a *prior appropriation* state, meaning "water rights are granted according to when a person applies a particular quantity of water to a beneficial use" (Getches 1990, 74). A user's entitlement to water is based on the date of the first appropriation of that water, that is, "first in time, first in right." Under this system there are three elements that make up a valid appropriation: intent, diversion, and beneficial use (75).

*Intent* implies that the user is going to put a quantity of water to beneficial use "within a reasonable time, using reasonable diligence" (76). Water is a precious commodity in an arid region such as Colorado, and the disuse of a water right will result in the loss of that right so another user may put that quantity of water to beneficial use. Maintaining a water right, then, requires a user such as the City of Aurora to apply "reasonable diligence" to some type of project, whether the water is actually needed at the present time or not. One may not sit idly on a water right without risking forfeiture of that right (77).

*Diversion* requires a user to remove a quantity of water from its natural state, and transport it to its site of *beneficial use*. A prior appropriation state generally does not prefer one beneficial use over another based on economics or social usefulness, but simply demands that the water be put to some beneficial use. As Getches notes: "The right to use water does not include the right to waste it" (ibid.), but it does require diligence in applying the water to some use. It is not difficult to see how a local municipality can easily demonstrate a beneficial use when it serves the water needs of its citizenry.

The right to pump groundwater from an aquifer, the storage facility in a conjunctive use project, is not so easily defined in a prior appropriation state. Allocation of rights based solely on prior use is not practical because *any* additional pumping causes some effect on the resource, either in quantity, quality or both aspects, and a senior user could theoretically disallow any junior appropriations (250). In order to remedy this situation, the State of Colorado, in its Groundwater Management Act of 1965, mandated a modified appropriation doctrine, which denies junior water rights only when the pumping of groundwater results in "the unreasonable lowering of the water level, or the unreasonable deterioration of the water quality, beyond reasonable economic limits of withdrawal or use" (265). Unreasonable harm is determined on a site-specific basis using geologic conditions, average annual yield and recharge rate of the groundwater supply, priority, and other criteria. It also requires that existing well owners have reasonably deep and efficient wells. Given this "vague statutory mandate" (266), as Getches calls it, the owners of existing wells in South Park have very little chance of getting a sympathetic ear in the state capital until such time as the quantity and/or quality of their water supply is "unreasonably harmed" by the actions of the City of Aurora as a junior appropriator of the South Park aquifer.

## CONJUNCTIVE USE

The term "conjunctive use" refers to the joint use of both subterranean and surface water resources, especially when the two resources are hydrologically interconnected (276). Often the surface resource is used to recharge the groundwater resource. This may be achieved through the augmentation of natural recharge through the importation of additional surface water, or it may be injected directly into the aquifer, or it may be spread out on the land overlying the aquifer in order to speed the recharge process (287-288).

In Colorado, conjunctive use projects are regulated by the Water Rights Determination and Administration Act of 1969 through the Act's *augmentation plans*. Under this legislation, junior appropriators can satisfy senior appropriation rights by preparing and implementing a plan for augmenting an aquifer through new diversion and storage facilities, development of new sources of water, and other groundwater augmentation schemes. Augmentation plans are subject to approval by the Colorado State Engineer (282).

## THE SOUTH PARK CONJUNCTIVE USE PROJECT

To date, the City of Aurora has produced two mailings to interested Park County residents and property owners. These mailings have included a letter from Tom Griswold, Director of Utilities for the City of Aurora, two Community Bulletins answering questions that have been asked in the *South Park Republican* and *Fairplay Flume* newspapers, and several color maps detailing the project and its location in the South Park basin. The following description of the South Park Conjunctive Use Project utilizes the information provided by the City of Aurora in these two mailings.

According to Griswold, the project represents an "alternative to expand Aurora's water supply in future years" (Griswold 1996, 1). The City expects to store 140,000 acre-feet of water in the South Park aquifer, and divert 20,000 acre-feet per year once the project is fully operational in 6-10 years. The aquifer itself is formed by the Elkhorn Thrust Fault, which creates a natural underground reservoir estimated at 100 square miles in area, 6000 feet in depth, and containing 16 million acre-feet of water. The project will require 26 well sites and 6 recharge reservoirs located on the Sportsmen's Ranch property, which has already been purchased by the City (*City of Aurora* 1996a, 1-3).

The City's research into stream flows in Tarryall Creek, Michigan Creek, and Park Gulch reveal the "cyclical nature of precipitation in the South Park area," and "show that over the past 47 years water would have been available for recharge to the aquifer two-thirds of the time" (*City of Aurora* 1996b, 3). The water "available for recharge" is a combination of natural runoff that flows through intermittent streams on Sportsmen's Ranch, and water that would be diverted from Tarryall Creek through a series of ditches to carry the water about two miles south to the recharge reservoirs.

When asked about the environmental impacts of the project, the City responded, "The environmental impacts are positive." It then goes on to say that Aurora's policy "discouraging the mining of groundwater" and Colorado water law will work to protect the South Park aquifer. In fact, the project will "increase stream flows and create small surface reservoirs; thereby enhancing fisheries, wildlife habitat and wetlands" (*City of Aurora* 1996a, 3).

## ETHICAL ANALYSIS

In order to analyze any project having to do with Colorado water law from the perspective of ethics, one must first turn back to John Locke, seventeenth-century English philosopher, and founder of our current understanding of property rights. According to Joseph des Jardins, Locke's "state of nature" argument has three parts:

1. A person has exclusive rights over his or her own body and its labor.
2. Land, in its natural state is unowned, i.e., no individual can claim exclusive control over it.
3. When one's own labor is "mixed" with unowned land, the exclusive rights of his or her labor are transferred to the land such that one then owns that piece of land (des Jardins 1993, 36).

Compare Locke's argument to the conditions for water rights under Colorado's prior appropriation doctrine. Recall that appropriation requires intent, diversion, and beneficial use on the part of the seeker of a water right. Recall further that intent requires *reasonable diligence*. In other words, the right to a quantity of water *as property* requires one to mix one's own labor with that water. The appropriation also requires *diversion*, the evidence of having applied labor to a quantity of water, and *beneficial use*, the work that the labor of acquiring the water right is intended to augment. Once one has applied the proper amount of labor to a quantity of water, one may be said to own that water regardless of the needs of others or any ecological harm that may come about as a result of obtaining the water.

Along with Locke's profoundly influential theory of property rights, we in the U.S. are greatly swayed by the utilitarian tradition. Utilitarianism may be summed up simply by the phrase "the greatest good for the greatest number" (29). Within this framework, one is acting ethically when the consequences of one's acts tend to maximize some "good" for as many people as possible. Note that "good" refers only to *people*. The utilitarian tradition has nothing to say regarding any "good" that may be gained or lost by individuals of non-human species, communities of species, or even entire ecosystems. It is completely anthropocentric and individualistic. It looks only for *the greatest good for the greatest number of people.*

The City of Aurora's South Park Conjunctive Use Project is a classic case study in the acquirement of property rights under the utilitarian tradition. In his letter to South Park property owners, Griswold states: "At this point, because of the requirements of the water court system, Aurora has made the necessary legal filings" (Griswold 1996, 1). Aurora has also been conducting research as noted above in its review of state records of stream flows in Tarryall Creek, Michigan Creek, and Park Gulch. Furthermore, the City is currently conducting infiltration tests on the Sportsmen's Ranch site of the project to determine whether the proposed reservoirs can actually recharge the South Park aquifer at the rate required by Aurora's demands. All of this points to a great deal of effort on the part of the City of Aurora to show *reasonable diligence* in its intent to create a diversion of a quantity of water. In doing so, Aurora can lay claim to that quantity of water -- not only under Colorado water law, but also under the theory of property rights so intrinsically understood by American society today.

And the City of Aurora plans to put that quantity of water to a *beneficial use* that far exceeds the use to which it is currently appropriated. No longer will that water sit idle. It will no longer be there merely for quenching the thirst of a few part-time residents or a few thousand head of cattle. No. That water will be used by thousands upon thousands of people seeking the good life in Aurora, Colorado. The utilitarian function is thus heavily weighted on the side of the City of Aurora, and the beneficial use to which it plans to put that quantity of water.

## THE QUESTION OF RISK

The first question posed by this essay is that of the ethics of imposing the risks of using an untested conjunctive use technology upon a local water supply that is wholly dependent on groundwater. For a different perspective on the question of risk, Aaron Wildavsky's *Searching for Safety* has been recommended. First, an explanation of Wildavsky's thoughts on risk, followed by application to the South Park Conjunctive Use Project.

Wildavsky takes William Rowe's definition for risk, which is "the potential for harm," or the probability of "negatively-valued events" (Wildavsky 1988, 3). The trick, says Wildavsky, "is to discover not how to avoid risk, for this is impossible, but how to use risk to get more of the good and less of the bad" (5). He goes on to suggest that society should actually pursue risky ventures in order to gain wisdom in how to get more of the good and less of the bad. He states:

*If all things are potentially risky, losses here may be made up by gains there. Advantages in one place may be given up in another. [...] The difficulty lies in advancing the whole so that more people are gaining than losing at any one time* (12-13).

This is quite clearly a utilitarian approach to the question of risk. It could easily be summed up in the phrase "the greatest good for the greatest number." It refers only to people, and in fact could be said to apply only to people who are currently alive since any risk to the potentially near-infinite numbers of people in future generations would obviously outweigh any advantage to even the billions of people currently inhabiting the planet. One could probably go a bit further and say that it applies only to people about whom one *cares.* Wildavsky apparently has no qualms against advantaging one set of people (the more numerous -- and chances are the risktaker is situated among the more numerous) over another.

Wildavsky goes on to contrast a strategy of "trial and error" against the illusory doctrine of "trial without error." He leans on Joseph Marone and Edward Woodhouse for their description of trial-and-error strategy: "(1)

establish a policy, (2) observe the effects, (3) correct for undesired effects, (4) observe the effects of the correction, and (5) correct again" (17). Pure incrementalism. Nothing but muddling through. Too bad if you happen to suffer any "undesired effects." It is especially too bad if you happen to be among some minority not advantaged by the policy. And what if there *is no correction* for the undesired effects, as we are currently facing in the possibilities of environmental disasters such as global warming from the rapid accumulation of greenhouse gases, or destruction of the ozone layer by man-made chemical compounds?

Admittedly, "trial without error," in which "no change whatsoever will be allowed unless there is solid proof that the proposed substance or action will do no harm" (ibid.), is an impossibly difficult standard for the policymaker to attain. As Wildavsky explains, a key assumption of those who would advocate no trials without prior guarantees of success is that the sources of safety and the sources of risk are separate and known. *Independent causation*, then, requires only that one choose sources of safety and reject sources of risk (42). Unfortunately, such a state of independent causation is nonexistent. We, in fact, move and make policy within a state of *interdependent causation*, in which "safety must be searched for indirectly, through processes that will lead to more good (and less bad) health effects" (ibid.). Here is the crux of the argument for Wildavsky: that people must continually and actively seek out those sources of safety in which the greatest good is produced for the greatest number of people. It is almost reminiscent of John Locke again in its requirement for *mixing one's own labor* with the property of safety in the utilitarian goals of current policymaking.

Wildavsky takes exception to the argument of some environmental economists who "would opt for the standard of efficiency called *Pareto optimality*, under which actions are justified if they make some people better off without harming others. But this criterion assumes, erroneously, that it is possible to separate harmful from beneficial effects" (18). And this is precisely where Wildavsky's argument falls apart. He is absolutely correct that all actions are interdependent, and that it is not possible to separate harmful from beneficial effects. But his conclusion that we must then continually and actively pursue risky ventures can only lead to greater harm to somebody or something, somewhere, at some point in time. Witness the greater harm of potential increases in ultraviolet radiation due to the luxury and convenience, even relative safety, of the use of chlorofluorocarbons in refrigeration and air conditioning. Here we have a case in which vast numbers of people in the future may be adversely affected by the search for safety (and luxury and convenience) on the part of a much smaller number of people living in the present. In fact, it may come to be said that the world would be a better place if we had not sought out the cooling properties of chlorofluorocarbons, but had instead used less dangerous chemicals or had simply chosen smarter alternatives such as not living in the desert if one is going to be intolerant of heat.

Application of Wildavsky's argument to the South Park Conjunctive Use Project is easy, and so is application of its counter. The City of Aurora can predict that sometime in the future it will see water shortages come from its current 1.8% annual growth rate. Aurora is situated in a semi-arid region, and has already exceeded the very limited supply of water it can take from streams and aquifers that flow within the city limits. Wildavsky would say that because Aurora is a city of many thousands of people, the good they will gain from the acquisition of water from the South Park aquifer far exceeds the good that may be had from that same source of water by a few part-time residents and a bunch of cattle. Further, he would say that the City is correct to risk adverse effects to the water supply for those South Park residents simply on *the chance* that the residents of Aurora may gain from the project, and even if it fails and the residents of South Park are harmed by the action, Wildavsky would say that the knowledge gained from the experiment is worth the damage done.

It is not difficult to argue that Wildavsky is wrong when applied to the South Park Conjunctive Use Project. As noted above, *any* pumping of an aquifer adversely affects the quantity and/or quality of water available for all other users of the aquifer. Pareto optimality would hold that the City of Aurora has no right to pursue water underlying the residents of South Park, knowing that it *will* adversely affect that population's water supply. And as far as Wildavsky's notion of the good in gaining knowledge from the project is concerned: *knowledge simply does not make a good substitute for water.*

## THE QUESTION OF SUSTAINABILITY

Sustainable development was defined by the World Commission on Environment and Development in its 1987 report called *Our Common Future.*

As summarized by Richard J. Tobin, "sustainable development requires meeting the essential needs of the present generation for food, clothing, shelter, jobs, and health without 'compromising the ability of future generations to meet their own needs'" (Tobin 1994, 276). On the surface, it would seem that the City of Aurora is doing its best to "meet the essential needs of the present generation" through the South Park Conjunctive Use Project. Indeed, it would seem to be doing this without even "compromising the ability of future generations to meet their own needs" if the project succeeds as proposed. But these statements are true *only* on the surface, and *only* when viewed through the lens of the utilitarian tradition. One must dig deeper, employing more recent developments in ethical analysis, to discover that the City of Aurora is not merely risking the environmental and economic well-being of South Park residents, but is risking the well-being of its own residents as well.

Two of the relatively recent developments in ethical analysis that can be applied to this situation are appropriate technology and social ecology. This next section will first look at the merits of each of these tools in environmental ethics, then apply them to the South Park Conjunctive Use Project.

## APPROPRIATE TECHNOLOGY

Appropriate technology is "the practice of matching needs with a specific technology that is most suitable for those needs" (des Jardins 1993, 237). It requires that we use the least energy-intensive, least environmentally damaging, and least costly methods of achieving a given goal. However, appropriate technology has implications not normally considered within standard utilitarian thinking: it implies the use of decentralized technologies, and it implies setting limits on the "needs" to which technology is applied.

First, the question of centralized vs. decentralized technologies. Centralized technologies require massive projects such as the diversion of water from its source, often many miles away, to our water faucets, swimming pools, and electrical generating plants in the semi-arid and desert regions that we insist on occupying. These massive projects require huge economic investment, and have altered the landscape forever with their attendant dams and flooded valleys. They invariably result in massive bureaucracies, both public sector and private, that arise insidiously and unannounced to seemingly take control of our lives, leaving us feeling helpless and at their mercy.

And we *are* at their mercy. We have left ourselves very vulnerable. Vulnerable to everything from natural disaster to technological failure to malicious attack. A prolonged series of dry years in the Colorado Rocky Mountains, and residents in the semi-arid Front Range of Colorado are suddenly faced with severely diminished quality of life, even life-threatening drought.

But it need not be this way. In fact, the story of South Park v. the City of Aurora is a case in point. The residents of South Park enjoy decentralized water technology in that each resident must acquire the water required for survival by obtaining water rights, then diverting a quantity of water for some beneficial use, usually residential or agricultural, normally through the construction of a well tapped into the South Park aquifer. Each resident is economically responsible for whatever costs this diversion may require.

The residents of Aurora, on the other hand, are living at the mercy of nature, technology, and the decision-making capabilities of the City Utilities Department. Their water comes from many miles away, in fact they probably do not even know *where* it comes from. If asked, most residents would probably say "the faucet." A prolonged series of dry years on the Continental Divide may render the abilities of Aurora to quench its thirst severely curtailed. A technological failure in a project such as the South Park Conjunctive Use Project could have equally disastrous results for the residents of Aurora.

All of which brings up the second point implied in appropriate technology -- that of limiting our perceived "needs." Read carefully Aldo Leopold's famous opening lines in "Good Oak" from *A Sand County Almanac*:

*There are two spiritual dangers in not owning a farm. One is the danger of supposing that breakfast comes from the grocery, and the other that heat comes from the furnace* (Leopold 1949, 6).

Here, Leopold is speaking directly to the question of centralized v. decentralized technologies. The farmer, in Leopold's ideal a self-sufficient producer of the requirements of life, not only knows exactly where breakfast and heat (and water) come from, but is also intimately aware of the amount of work required to bring these essential components into the farmhouse where they can be utilized by the farmer's family. These necessities are not wasted frivolously because their consumption so immediately results in additional back-breaking labor. Decentralized technologies require this kind of intimate knowledge of one's own habits of consumption. If one wants eggs for breakfast, one must raise, feed, and water some chickens. If one wants to heat one's home, one must spend considerable time chopping wood. One does not merely order an egg or turn up the thermostat. It forces one to make consumption decisions at the personal and local level. If one's water needs are met solely by one's own well, in which the flow of water is directly proportional to the amount of money and labor invested in the well's depth and pumping apparatus, one must think twice about that jacuzzi spa bathtub. And a similar set of considerations is required at the local level, where the aggregate of these individual decisions must be handled. Des Jardins writes:

*Of equal importance is the fact that appropriate technologies can also foster democratic virtues. Decentralized technologies support a process of localized decision making in a way that complex and bureaucratic technologies do not* (des Jardins 1993, 238).

Because each of the residents of South Park is intimately aware of their water consumption and the costs incurred to secure that water, they are collectively able to manage the local water resource more effectively. They will self-impose limits on the use of that resource because each of them is vitally interested in the maintenance of its continued viability. When the resource can no longer support additional users, the local community will impose restrictions on additional permits to the resource.

The residents of Aurora cannot perform this function of self-governance. Because they do not know where their water comes from or how it gets to the faucet, they have no knowledge of the limitations of the resource. They also, then, have no reason to monitor their own consumption or the consumption of others in their community. They must rely wholly upon the wisdom of their public officials for advice as to when to conserve water. Yet, when such conservation is mandated, they feel powerless and deprived of their right to the lifestyle they were promised. Most importantly, they have no reason to question the rate of population growth in the City of Aurora, and that leads directly into the relatively recent development of social ecology in the ethical analysis of environmental problems.

Social ecology is largely concerned with the hierarchies found in society, and their effects on the society and its constituents. It is based to a great extent on the ideas put forward by Murray Bookchin, a social theorist, in his book, *The Ecology of Freedom*. Bookchin equates the hierarchies found in society with systematic domination of one group over another based on age, gender, ethnicity, wealth, knowledge, and any number of other factors that contribute to power in a society (242-243). An example of hierarchy in the society of the City of Aurora was described above, in which a great deal of power is held by those who dole out the water supply. No such hierarchy is found in the South Park community, where individual water users each have the knowledge and interest required to govern their own water usage. The residents of Aurora feel powerless in terms of water usage *because they are powerless.*

Social ecology is especially applicable to undertakings such as the South Park Conjunctive Use Project, in which we see the domination of one community by another. In our society, it is common for larger municipalities to dominate smaller municipalities. Because the utilitarian tradition promotes "the greatest good for the greatest number of people," larger communities can assert themselves based simply on the "greater good" they are seeking. The City of Aurora can impose itself upon the community of South Park residents because the "beneficial use" to which Aurora can divert the South Park aquifer is so much "greater" according to utilitarian thinking. Which leads to a great deal of competition among municipalities to dominate more and more water resources at greater and greater distances from their intended beneficial use. All of which leads to statements such as this one by Tom Griswold of the City of Aurora: *If Aurora had not purchased this project, some other entity would have* (Griswold 1996, 1). Now *there's* a good reason for putting South Park at risk for environmental degradation, economic hardship, and the unrecoverable loss of its underlying aquifer!

## CONCLUSIONS

The detrimental aspects of the City of Aurora's South Park Conjunctive Use Project thus fall into two categories: harms to South Park, and harms to the City of Aurora. First, a look at potential harm to South Park.

The South Park Conjunctive Use Project is a proposal to alter the ecosystem of South Park. Aurora's Griswold calls it "an opportunity to develop a water project in an environmentally sensitive manner which could in fact increase wetlands, low flow season stream flows, and fisheries" (ibid.). These "improvements" are based on wholly anthropocentric considerations of what is good in an ecosystem. The fact is, South Park is a semi-arid intermountain valley. It is a place of few wetlands, intermittent streams, and little in the way of fisheries. It maintains its own ecosystem "goods," and they have everything to do with the fact that there is precious little surface water. Its beauty lies largely in its austerity of life. It is a hard beauty, untempered by the ease of abundantly available surface water. Introduction of surface reservoirs to the South Park valley floor for the benefit of the City of Aurora and others who seek anthropocentric goods where they do not currently exist would result in irreparable damage to the present ecosystem and its own set of environmental goods.

The potential harm to South Park residents through the degradation of their only water supply is obvious. Should the South Park Conjunctive Use Project result in loss of quantity or quality of water to the residents of South Park, the impact on the local community may be severe. Griswold states, "If there are adverse impacts to existing rights due to Aurora's project, they will be fully mitigated" (2). Unfortunately, *money is a poor substitute for water.*

And the City of Aurora faces its own set of harms as well. Its reliance on centralized technologies such as the South Park Conjunctive Use Project leave its residents with little margin in times of drought. Should the project fail to deliver the quantity of water required by the City, the residents of Aurora have then invested their hopes for future water supplies, and a good deal of money, in a fragile scheme that did not deliver as promised.

But it is the City of Aurora's insistence on continued growth that is setting it up for disaster. The South Park Conjunctive Use Project is purportedly not required for the current population of Aurora, but is "an alternative to expand the City's water supply in future years" (1). As Aurora continues to grow at "a moderate annual growth rate of 1.8%" (*City of Aurora* 1996a, 4), and reaches ever further and further away from its city limits to obtain water for those future residents, it risks greater and greater calamity for itself should those sources of water become scarce.

## RECOMMENDATIONS

The City of Aurora would thus do well to adhere to the philosophies of deep ecology, as here summarized by des Jardins:

*Deep ecologists are committed to promoting lifestyles that "tread lightly on the Earth." This means that humans ought to live in simple, relatively nontechnological, self-reliant, decentralized communities* (des Jardins 1993, 231).

The City of Aurora should question its motives and its actions in its proposed South Park Conjunctive Use Project. It should question the utilitarian tradition on which it is basing its quest for water to serve the "greater good." It should question the anthropocentric "good" it seeks to impose upon the South Park ecosystem, forever altering a set of environmental goods that already lie in exquisitely harmonious balance, and are profoundly beautiful in and of themselves. It should question its reliance on centralized technologies that serve to increase the risk of failure, and continually diminish its residents' ability to act in a democratically sound manner. It should question the domination of other, smaller communities in the full realization that hierarchy is a state of consciousness as well as a social condition. Again, des Jardins:

*Humans can go through life being created by and in turn creating their social world without fully recognizing this reality, or they can be fully conscious of and responsible for this history* (245).

The City of Aurora should look to South Park, not for water, but for examples in how to manage itself in ways that are environmentally and ethically sound. The City of Aurora should cease and desist further work on its proposed South Park Conjunctive Use Project.

## CRITICAL THINKING DRILLS

1. Apply John Locke's "state of nature" argument to our current notion of property rights. How is it that we "mix our labor" with various types of properties such that we can call them our own?

2. Think about the utilitarian argument made by Aaron Wildavsky concerning the question of risk. Does it sound fair to you? Can you propose a better solution to the problem of risk?

3. Do you agree that the City of Aurora should discontinue its plans for a conjunctive use project? Why or why not? Which of the several arguments made in this essay best explains your own conclusion?

## RESEARCH FOR THE ADVENTUROUS

Research the idea of *sustainable development*. Write a 600-word essay critiquing sustainable development, citing recent examples of attempts to implement such a strategy as arguments for or against your own conclusion.

## REFERENCES

City of Aurora. April 15, 1996. "Community Bulletin #1."

City of Aurora. Summer 1996. "Community Bulletin."

des Jardins, J. R. 1993. Environmental Ethics. Belmont, CA: Wadsworth Publishing Company.

Getches, D. H. 1990. *Water Law in a Nutshell*. St. Paul, MN: West Publishing

Griswold, T. April 19, 1996. "Letter to Park County Property Owners."

Leopold, A. 1949. *A Sand County Almanac*. New York: Oxford University Press.

Tobin, R. J. 1994. "Environment, Population, and Economic Development." *Environmental Policy in the 1990s*. Norman J. Vig and Michael E. Kraft, eds. 1994. Washington, D.C.: Congressional Quarterly Press.

Wildavsky, A. B. 1988. *Searching for Safety*. New Brunswick: Transaction Books.

# HUMAN POPULATION GROWTH

*The environmentalist is often presented with questions concerning the rapid growth of the human population. What is the carrying capacity for humans on planet Earth? This essay briefly defines carrying capacity, then offers a non-biological theory of human population growth.*

The curve for human growth is thought to be a logistic, or S-shaped, curve as found in numerous other K-strategists, those species that maintain their densest populations at the carrying capacity of their environment (Smith 1992, 209). At this point, however, such thinking is speculative: while human population growth was indeed flat prior to 8000 B.C., and has risen exponentially since then, we really have no way of knowing whether we are at the planet's carrying capacity or not. We may have already exceeded carrying capacity and now find ourselves in the "overshoot" portion of our growth curve as it declines then flattens out. Or we may be nowhere near the peak of our population.

We see all of the mechanisms of population regulation at work. The urban middle class of North America has been at zero population growth for sometime, but is it stress-induced decreases in births, or is it higher education and dual incomes? Dispersal has encouraged "white flight" from the cities to the suburbs, and "brain drain" from the Third World to the New World. Nationalism is nothing more nor less than territoriality, with its characteristic song and call heard in our national anthems, and intimidation displays seen in military exercises conducted just outside the national borders of our rivals. Occasionally, when resources are thought to be unfairly distributed, we make war.

I would submit that *homo sapiens* is constantly at carrying capacity, yet we are nowhere near the peak of our population. We have learned to harness the increased carrying capacities of agriculture, trade, the Industrial Age, education, the Green Revolution, and the Information Age. We have yet to fully tap the carrying capacities implied by space travel, wisdom or even science, genuine civilization, peace on Earth, or any of the as-yet unimagined human advances toward truth, beauty and goodness awaiting us in the future.

## CRITICAL THINKING DRILLS

1.  Do you think the human population has reached the carrying capacity of the planet? Give examples to defend your argument.

2.  How should human population best be controlled if and when it reaches the carrying capacity of Earth?

## RESEARCH FOR THE ADVENTUROUS

Review the literature on *life history strategies* from an ecologist's perspective. Apply the definitions of *r*-strategists and *K*-strategists to *homo sapiens* and write a brief summary of how our species' survival depends on our application of a life history strategy that is unique to humans.

## REFERENCES

Smith, R. L. 1992. *Elements of Ecology*. New York: HarperCollins Publishing.

# MANAGING PLANET EARTH

*The environmentalist, in the course of argument, may become entangled in the web of so-called sustainable development policies. What are sustainable development policies? This critique of William C. Clark's Scientific American article of the same name concludes that they are personal, and based upon individuals having enough education and information to make sound decisions supportive of sustainable-development objectives.*

In a *Scientific American* publication titled "Managing Planet Earth," William C. Clarke states that the first requirement for sustainable development policies is making information on which people "base their decisions more supportive of sustainable-development objectives" (Clark 1990, 9). I believe this is imperative. While I must admit that my own patterns of consumption and disposal are not perfect (see "A Day in the Life," below) I will claim that they are far superior to the average of my Western cohort of the late 20th Century. My decisions are based on a dynamic data set, from which I critically determine how to proceed with the least impact upon the planet. Without the education that I have received and continue to seek, I could never make these informed decisions, and would be forced to rely solely on media images telling me how to eat, dress, buy, and interact with my peers.

Clarke states that a second requirement "for adaptive planetary management is the invention and implementation of technologies for sustainable development" (ibid.). I believe this is a goal we should all be working toward, but it is not a requirement. We must learn to use current technologies in sustainable ways. Although I believe we will see many more such inventions in our own lifetimes, we must learn not to rely on them. They should each be a pleasant surprise, not the long hoped-for solution to some pressing problem.

Finally, Clarke writes, "A third requirement for adaptive planetary management is the construction of mechanisms at the national and international level to coordinate managerial activities." (10). I believe this is a step in the right direction, but the ultimate policy of sustainable development will come only from within a planetary government, that has as its constituents a highly educated populace, able to speak one another's languages fluently, and free from national envy and social prejudice. To the 20th Century mind it will look like heaven on earth.

## CRITICAL THINKING DRILLS

1. Is sustainable development a personal issue, as argued above, or is it actually a model of development that can be determined by scientists and engineers?

2. What role does education play in the potential for sustainable development? Consider negative connotations, such as increased consumption and pollution on the part of well educated societies, as well as seemingly positive connotations such as lower birth rates among educated women.

## RESEARCH FOR THE ADVENTUROUS

Research the literature on sustainable development and write your own 600-word assessment of the state of the art.

## REFERENCES

Clark, W. C. 1990. "Managing Planet Earth." *Managing Planet Earth: Readings from Scientific American Magazine*. New York: W.H. Freeman and Company.

# STRATEGIES FOR AGRICULTURE

*The environmentalist may specifically become ensnared by the question of sustainable agriculture. How can sustainable development policies be applied to strategies for agriculture? This essay first looks to Aldo Leopold for framing the question in a manner that is intensely personal, then places the burden for feeding the world on the backs of each and every one of us.*

*There are two spiritual dangers in not owning a farm. One is the danger of supposing that breakfast comes from the grocery, and the other that heat comes from the furnace.*

*To avoid the first danger, one should plant a garden, preferably where there is no grocer to confuse the issue.*

*To avoid the second, he should lay a split of good oak on the andirons, preferably where there is no furnace, and let it warm his shins while a February blizzard tosses the trees outside. If one has cut, split, hauled, and piled his own good oak, and let his mind work the while, he will remember much about where the heat comes from, and with a wealth of detail denied to those who spend the weekend in town astride a radiator.* (Leopold 1949, 6)

In another *Scientific American* article, titled "Strategies for Agriculture," Pierre R. Crosson and Norman J. Rosenberg state that "the challenge to agriculture is not only to provide food for the 10 billion people who will probably be living a century from now but also to achieve that level of production with less environmental damage than is apparent today" (Crosson & Rosenberg 1990, 78). While these goals are indeed important, no, *vital* to the continued human population growth that they predict, this is really only the beginning of what sustainable agriculture must do for mankind. As Leopold said, "land yields a cultural harvest" (Leopold 1949, ix).

While agricultural technology may be able to feed us when we are 10 billion in number, it will only contribute to our dispossession of the planet. Multiple cropping and Integrated Pest Management will undoubtedly feed billions of mouths, but they will never feed a single soul. Removal of water subsidies in an attempt to force farmers to use water conservation techniques may save water, but they will not in themselves convince the farmer and the beneficiaries of agriculture of the duty we each bear to enhance our planet through our presence, not consume and pollute it. "The emerging social scarcities of land, water and genetic diversity" (Crosson & Rosenberg 1990, 83) are not the purview of "institutional mechanisms" as claimed by Crosson and Rosenberg -- they are the planetary realities that must be borne by each and every one of us, every waking moment of our lives. When we have learned this lesson, we will have achieved the goals of sustainable agriculture.

## CRITICAL THINKING DRILLS

1.  Critique Aldo Leopold's statement regarding "spiritual dangers" at the beginning of this essay. What danger is there in remaining oblivious to where your food, water, and energy come from? How should we confront this problem in the United States?

2.  How can each of us bear responsibility for the agricultural practices used to provide us with our nutritional requirements? What role should industry play? The government?

## RESEARCH FOR THE ADVENTUROUS

Read Leopold's "Foreword" in *A Sand County Almanac*. Describe in 600 words the "cultural harvest" that Leopold alludes to.

# REFERENCES

Crosson, P. R. and Rosenberg, N. J. 1990. "Strategies for Agriculture." *Managing Planet Earth: Readings from Scientific American Magazine.* New York: W.H. Freeman and Company.

Leopold, A. 1949. *A Sand County Almanac.* New York: Oxford University Press.

# "DOLLARS AND CENTS:" A HIGHER STANDARD?

*The environmentalist is often presented with epidemiological analysis, in which strong correlations may be used to link environmental hazards with specific human diseases. In June 1995, the American Lung Association released a study called "Dollars and Cents: The Economic and Health Benefits of Potential Particulate Matter Reductions in the United States." The report was written by Lauraine G. Chestnut of Hagler Bailly Consulting, Inc. of Boulder, Colorado. This review takes issue with several of Chestnut's assumptions, but generally applauds the work as a necessary wake-up call for the public and its elected officials regarding atmospheric particulate matter pollution in the United States.*

## INTRODUCTION

Americans are literally choking on the minute particles kicked up into the atmosphere by automobiles, buses and trucks, construction activity, and coal-fired electrical generating plants. At the same time, state and local legislative bodies are choking on the standards currently in place to reduce particulate matter in the air we breathe, particularly that of $PM_{10}$ (particulate matter less than 10 microns in diameter).

It seems nobody likes the current standards. Business interests and conservative legislators are attempting to relax the standards, which are set by the Environmental Protection Agency (EPA) but implemented at the state level. Environmentalists and health organizations are trying to get *stricter* standards adopted, even in non-attainment areas that do not meet the current standards. Are the current standards too tough or too loose? Are the standards fine just the way they are? It is quite possible our attention to the standards themselves is misguided.

Chestnut concludes in *Dollars and Cents: The Economic and Health Benefits of Potential Particulate Matter Reductions in the United States,* that the U.S. could reduce health care expenditures due to inhalation of $PM_{10}$ by an additional \$10.9 billion each year if the nation were to adopt a National Ambient Air Quality Standard (NAAQS) for $PM_{10}$ as stringent as that of California. The report is well-written and thoroughly researched. It reaches satisfying conclusions based on the assumptions that are made, and thoroughly explained, throughout. There are three features of the report that merit critical review: 1) the use of epidemiological analysis on which the report's conclusions are based; 2) the use of willingness-to-pay assumptions in calculating monetary outcomes; and 3) Chestnut's recommendation that stricter standards for $PM_{10}$ be adopted throughout the U.S.

## EPIDEMIOLOGY

Critics of Chestnut's report have found her use of epidemiological analysis inadmissible to any discussion of alleviating local air pollution problems involving $PM_{10}$. This is clearly unfortunate, and leads to ill-considered ranting such as this one, put forth by Al Knight, Perspective Editor for The Denver Post:

*Buried in the report is this admission. "The exact biological mechanism that underlies the observed epidemiological association have [sic] not been established." What that means is that scientists don't agree there is a mechanism by which a specific level of fine particulates causes illness or shortens life. The study does not, and cannot, demonstrate that air pollution is responsible for specific deaths or specific hospital admissions.*

*Statistical correlations can be found everywhere. Some are important, some not* (Knight 1995, D-1).

And this one is important. Especially if you happen to live in a non-attainment zone for particulates. Even more so if you happen to be a child, asthmatic, elderly, or otherwise susceptible to respiratory ailments.

Epidemiology is the branch of science concerned with the occurrence, distribution, and determinants of states of health and disease in human populations (Abramson 1979, 7). It uses the power of statistical correlation to test cause-and-effect hypotheses that cannot be tested clinically, as is the case in particulate matter as a hypothesized cause of respiratory ailments in humans. It would be extremely difficult to clinically observe the effects of microscopic particles on lung tissue, especially in humans, but it is not difficult to find numerous statistically significant positive correlations between atmospheric particulates and respiratory ailments. In fact, "some of the most widely known findings in the epidemiology literature concern the respiratory effects (cancer, acute bronchitis, emphysema, the common cold, and pneumonia) of air pollution" (Crocker et al 1979, 4). And while it is true that epidemiological studies are capable of showing statistically significant correlation where there is no cause-effect relationship, one of the strengths of Chestnut's report is her very careful use of existing epidemiological analysis. She explains her reasons for including the studies she based her report on, and she also explains why she discarded a number of other studies. The reader predisposed to accepting the results of good analysis is left feeling satisfied that Chestnut's conclusions of a cause-effect relationship between $PM_{10}$ and health expenditures are valid. Mr. Knight probably scoffs at the notion of a correlation between smoking and lung cancer -- after all, a cause-effect relationship has never been clinically proven there either.

## WILLINGNESS TO PAY

Of the several assumptions that a report of this kind must make, it is Chestnut's use of willingness to pay (WTP) that leaves the reader feeling most unsure of her financial conclusions. Health care analysis often does not make conclusions based on ability to pay because "someone's ability to pay is only relevant for evaluations of policy if one can coerce the person into consuming the goods or services" (Gertler & van der Gaag 1990, 56-57). Rather, it attempts to find the public's *willingness to pay* for policies of increased health care through surveys and observation of consumption patterns.

Chestnut justifies her use of WTP by stating that "using COI [cost of illness] measures in a quantitative assessment results in a clear downward bias in the valuation of adverse health effects" (Chestnut 1995, 5-2). In fact, she adjusts all

COI figures upward by a factor of *two* to offset this "downward bias" (5-5). She arrived at the WTP factor used in her conclusions by analyzing the ranges of "value of a statistical life" (VSL) determined through several recent studies. She is careful to devote an entire chapter of the report to an explanation of her WTP estimates. Yet it does not convince.

The reader is left feeling Chestnut is straining at gnats and swallowing camels. Granted, the *$10.9 billion* savings in health care that Chestnut projects would not be possible without a WTP factor. But a report that based its conclusions solely on the actual costs incurred by respiratory ailments attributed to atmospheric particulate matter would be much easier to swallow.

## CHESTNUT'S RECOMMENDATION

Chestnut concludes that the U.S. would see an estimated $10.9 billion savings in health care expenditures if the nation were to adopt standards for $PM_{10}$ as strict as that of California. She, therefore, recommends adoption of California's stricter standards across the nation in order that we may benefit from this obviously "better" standard.

The problem lies in that there are many areas in the U.S. (including large parts of California) that cannot even meet the *current* standards as set by EPA. It would seem that Chestnut has placed the cart before the horse in calling for stricter standards when the current standards are as yet unattainable in the areas of the country with the worst $PM_{10}$ problems. She estimates (using WTP) we would see annual savings of $787 million if the entire nation were simply to meet the *current* standards for particulates. This is still a great deal of money: $786,800,000.00. While this figure may not have the headline-grabbing impact that $Billions and $Billions do, it does at least represent a more attainable goal. One that would make cost analysis of solutions to reduce $PM_{10}$ more plausible.

## CONCLUSIONS

This report is an admirable attempt to make real the costs of particulate matter in the air that we breathe as they pertain to health care. The author's use of epidemiological analysis is sound, and reaches important conclusions. These conclusions should be broadcast across the land as a call to arms in the fight against air pollution, specifically $PM_{10}$ pollution. Unfortunately, the impact of the report is lessened somewhat by the use of willingness-to-pay factors that make the final results soar into the realm of the unbelievable. And the report's recommendation for stricter standards in light of our inability to meet the current standards makes for sorry comment on the state of the art in environmental policy analysis.

We need solutions -- real, workable solutions -- to the problems of $PM_{10}$ and other forms of air pollution. We do not need more and more analysis telling us how much money we could save if we only had more standards, stricter standards.

Aaron Wildavsky said it best:

*Only by suggesting solutions [...] can we understand what might be done* (Wildavsky 1979, 26).

Standards are not solutions.

## CRITICAL THINKING DRILLS

1.   Research and discuss the arguments for and against the use of epidemiological analysis.

2.   How much should society spend in order to cleanse the atmosphere of particulate matter? Should it be equal to estimated savings in health care costs? More? Less? Justify your answer.

3.   Critique this essay's conclusion that "standards are not solutions." Do you agree or disagree with this statement? Why?

## RESEARCH FOR THE ADVENTUROUS

Write a 600-word summary of Aaron Wildavsky's solutions-based theory of policy analysis.

# REFERENCES

Abramson, J. H. 1979. *Survey Methods in Methods in Community Medicine.* New York:    Churchill Livingstone Inc.

Chestnut, L. G. 1995. "Dollars and Cents: The Economic and Health Benefits of Potential    Particulate Matter Reductions in the United States." New York: American Lung Association.

Crocker, T. D., Schulze, W., Ben-David, S., and Kneese, A. V. 1979. *Methods Development  for Assessing Air Pollution Control Benefits, Volume I.* Washington, D.C.: U.S. Environmental Protection Agency.

Gertler, P. and van der Gaag, J. 1990. *The Willingness to Pay for Medical Care.* Baltimore and London: The Johns Hopkins University Press;

Knight, A. July 2, 1995. "Interest Groups Emphasize Benefits and Ignore Costs." *The Denver Post.* Denver CO: The Denver Post

Wildavsky, A. B. 1979. *Speaking Truth to Power: The Art and Craft of Policy Analysis.* Boston, MA: Little, Brown Publishers.

# COST-EFFECTIVENESS ANALYSIS OF POLICY ALTERNATIVES TO REDUCE PM$_{10}$ IN THE DENVER METROPOLITAN NONATTAINMENT AREA

*The environmentalist may be required by policy makers to demonstrate the cost effectiveness of measures to reduce environmental hazards. In this essay, a number of solutions proposed to reduce Colorado's particulate matter problem are analyzed for cost effectiveness. They include expanded use of mass transit systems, use of liquids to melt snow and ice rather than the sand/salt mixture currently in use in most communities, and requiring electrical generating plants to switch from coal to natural gas. In this analysis, it is clear that reduced street sanding and restrictions on wood burning in the Denver area should not only reduce particulate matter pollution significantly, but also reduce the Brown Cloud and put money in our pockets at the same time. None of this has occurred, at least not so as to be noticed by the average citizen.*

## INTRODUCTION

The purpose of this essay is to utilize cost-effectiveness analysis in determining which of the proposed methods currently under consideration for reducing particulate matter pollution in the Denver Metropolitan Nonattainment Area would produce the greatest reduction in pollution for the least cost.

The Colorado Air Quality Control Commission (the Commission) stipulated, as the basis for this analysis, use of a report produced for the American Lung Association (ALA) titled *DOLLARS AND CENTS: The Economic and Health Benefits of Potential Particulate Matter Reductions in the United States* by Lauraine G. Chestnut of Hagler Bailly Consulting, Inc. of Boulder, Colorado. See "Dollars and Cents: A Higher Standard?," above.

## PARTICULATE MATTER AS AN ATMOSPHERIC POLLUTANT

Atmospheric particulate matter, also known as particulates, PMs, or total suspended particulate matter (TSP), is made up of carbon-based particles, dust, and acid aerosols. It can be produced naturally, but today is more often the result of diesel bus and truck emissions, factory and utility smokestacks, car exhaust, wood burning, mining, and construction activity (ALA 1994, 1). In Colorado, especially the Denver metropolitan area, the sanding of streets for vehicular traction under conditions of snow and ice is a significant contributor to the area's Brown Cloud during the winter months.

$PM_{10}$ is the term used to denote particles less than 10 microns in diameter. Particles this small are of special significance because they are able to remain suspended in the atmosphere for relatively long periods of time, and are easily inhaled deep into the lungs (ibid). In 1986, the Environmental Protection Agency (EPA) set the current National Ambient Air Quality Standard (NAAQS) for $PM_{10}$ at 150 micrograms per cubic meter ($\mu g/m^3$) averaged over 24 hours, and 50 $\mu g/m^3$ averaged over one year (ALA 1995, S-1). The Denver metropolitan area and several other Colorado communities are currently in nonattainment of the federal NAAQS for particulates.

A number of solutions to Colorado's particulate matter problem have been proposed. They include expanded use of mass transit systems, use of liquids to melt snow and ice rather than the sand/salt mixture currently in use in most communities, and requiring electrical generating plants to switch from coal to natural gas. According to Stacy Nutt, staff economist for the State of Colorado Air Pollution Control Division (APCD), the State Implementation Plan (SIP) for Colorado details the plans of nonattainment areas for reducing particulates in that area to the federal standards. This analysis will use the *Colorado State Implementation Plan for Particulate Matter ($PM_{10}$) Denver Metropolitan*

*Nonattainment Area Element* to analyze solutions proposed for the Denver nonattainment area.

# THE CONCEPT OF COST

Because *Dollars and Cents* uses cost analysis to recommend the adoption of stricter standards for particulate matter after meeting federal standards, this study makes further use of cost analysis in order to determine whether solutions proposed to bring Colorado into attainment on $PM_{10}$ are cost effective and will actually be cost beneficial in comparison to the benefits predicted by the ALA report. Any intervention in atmospheric pollution uses resources that could otherwise be utilized for other valued alternatives. "The value of what is given up or sacrificed represents the cost of an alternative" (Levin 1983, 48). Thus, this report must determine whether the health care savings predicted by *Dollars and Cents* will be outweighed by the cost of implementing any one of a number of alternative policies aimed at reducing $PM_{10}$ in Colorado.

# COST-EFFECTIVENESS ANALYSIS

Cost-effectiveness analysis (CEA) is a subset of cost-benefit analysis (CBA), which is the evaluation of alternatives by comparison of their associated costs and benefits when each is measured in monetary terms (Levin 1983, 21). Cost-benefit analysis sets out to determine the *efficiency*, that is, the ratio of inputs and outputs, of a given policy alternative (Brewer & deLeon 1983, 335). Cost-effectiveness, on the other hand, may be used to analyze policy alternatives in which efficiency and another goal, quantifiable but non-monetized, are of equal concern to the decision maker (Weimer & Vining 1992, 221).

So, where cost-benefit analysis is primarily concerned with efficiency, cost-effectiveness analysis is concerned with the *comparative effectiveness*, the ratio of observed output to planned output over some time period (Brewer & deLeon 1983, 338), *of multiple policy alternatives*. As Levin states: "When costs are combined with measures of effectiveness and all alternatives can be evaluated according to their costs and their contribution to meeting the same effectiveness criterion, we have the ingredients for a CEA analysis" (Levin 1983, 18). Two assumptions are made:

1. Only programs with similar or identical goals can be compared; and
2. A common measure of effectiveness can be used to assess them (ibid).

There are two approaches commonly taken in cost-effectiveness analysis --
*fixed budget* and *fixed effectiveness* (Weimer & Vining 1992, 221-222). In the
first approach, a decision maker has a certain level of funding that can be applied
to solving a problem, and cost-effectiveness analysis is used to determine which
of several alternatives will result in the most impact at that level of funding. In
the second approach, a decision maker desires a particular level of impact and
uses cost-effectiveness analysis to determine which of several alternatives will
achieve that level of impact for the least cost.

Cost-benefit analysis determines whether a policy alternative is worth doing
at all. By taking the ratio of outputs (benefits) to inputs (cost), CBA tells the
decision maker whether the desired outcome is worth the cost of achieving it --
provided both the inputs and the outputs can be monetized. A policy alternative
that has been deemed preferable through cost-effectiveness analysis may still fail
the efficiency test of cost-benefit analysis.

Thus cost analysis takes multiple forms, each with its own strengths and
weaknesses. The strengths and weaknesses of cost-effectiveness analysis are
given by Levin:

Strengths of cost-effectiveness analysis:

Merely requires combining cost data with effectiveness data
Lends itself well to an evaluation of alternatives that are being
considered for accomplishing a particular [...] goal
Weaknesses of cost-effectiveness analysis: (ibid)
Cannot compare alternatives with different goals
Cannot determine whether a program is worthwhile in the sense that its
benefits exceed its costs (Levin 1983, 21)

The use of cost-effectiveness analysis  can give the decision maker the
advantage of choosing an alternative that leads to a more efficient use of
resources. Using one of the two approaches discussed above, it can reduce the
cost of attaining a particular objective and it can expand what can be
accomplished with a given budget (11). Because it does not require that the
outcome be monetized, cost-effectiveness can use any quantifiable measure of

effectiveness. Because policy decisions must be based upon a demonstrated consideration of both the costs and effects of such decisions, cost-effectiveness analysis is a useful tool for comparing the effectiveness of multiple policy alternatives (ibid).

## COST-EFFECTIVENESS OF AIR QUALITY CONTROL MEASURES

Cost-effectiveness has a history of use in comparing air quality control policies. The measure of effectiveness generally used for these purposes is dollars per ton of pollutant eliminated (Suhrbier 1983, 5). Policy alternatives that have the single goal of reducing pollution emissions can be compared using the ratio of cost/ton of reduced emission. The decision maker can then use either the fixed budget approach to choose the alternative that reduces the most pollutant given the allotted funding, or the fixed effectiveness approach to reduce the emissions to the desired level using the least costly method. As Suhrbier states: "The major advantage in terms of air quality is that emissions do not have to be converted to air-quality levels, health, or dollars. These are controversial conversions, and it is nice to be able to avoid them" (ibid).

## USE OF COST-EFFECTIVENESS ANALYSIS IN PARTICULATE MATTER REDUCTION

Because there are numerous policy alternatives available to combat $PM_{10}$ in Colorado, cost-effectiveness analysis is a particularly useful tool with which to compare them, assuming the cost data are available. While some programs, such as increased use of mass transit systems, may have outcomes beyond reduction of $PM_{10}$ (for example, reduced traffic congestion and other pollutants) that are not attainable by programs such as reducing the amount of sanding of city streets, the programs may still be compared in respect to reduction of particulate matter because a common measure of effectiveness can be used to assess them, that of dollars per ton of reduced $PM_{10}$ in the atmosphere.

# USE OF COST-BENEFIT ANALYSIS IN PARTICULATE MATTER REDUCTION

After analyzing $PM_{10}$ reduction measures in terms of their cost-effectiveness, this report will make cost-benefit conclusions based on the conclusions reached in Chestnut's "Dollars and Cents" report produced for the American Lung Association.

Chestnut concludes that the U.S. would see an estimated $10.9 billion savings in health care expenditures if the nation were to adopt standards for $PM_{10}$ as strict as that of California. In reaching her conclusions, Chestnut demonstrates the Denver metropolitan area would see an estimated $192.5 million savings in health care expenditures if the nation were to attain the California standards for $PM_{10}$. The problem lies in that there are many areas in the U.S. (including the Denver Metropolitan Nonattainment Area) that do not meet the current standards as set by EPA. She estimates (using willingness-to-pay analysis) the nation would see annual savings of $787 million if the entire nation were to simply meet the current standards for particulates. The use of willingness-to-pay analysis is problematic in itself -- a critique of her willingness-to-pay analysis may be found in "Dollars and Cents: A Higher Standard?", above.

Unfortunately, Chestnut does not estimate the savings in health care expenditures that the Denver area would see if it were to meet the current EPA standards for particulates. Because this report is concerned with solutions proposed to meet the current standards in the Denver nonattainment area, it is not useful to compare the costs of those solutions with estimated health care savings obtained from stricter standards. In order to remedy this situation, this report will assume that the Denver area would see the same ratio of savings between meeting the current standards and attaining the stricter California standards that Chestnut estimates for the nation as a whole, that is, $786.8 million / $10.9 billion, or 0.0722. Applying this ratio to Chestnut's estimates for the Denver area results in savings in health care expenditures of $13.9 million. It is this estimated cost savings (benefit) to the Denver area that will be used to make cost-benefit comparisons in this analysis.

# THE COLORADO STATE IMPLEMENTATION PLAN FOR PARTICULATE MATTER: DENVER METROPOLITAN NONATTAINMENT AREA ELEMENT

The Colorado SIP for Denver presents the plan for reducing $PM_{10}$ pollution in the five-county Denver metropolitan area. Its primary focus is technical analysis, but it does provide some cost analysis as well. It is this cost analysis that will be featured in this discussion of solutions proposed for reducing particulates in Denver.

## ORGANIZATIONS INVOLVED IN PREPARING THE SIP

The SIP for $PM_{10}$ in the Denver Metropolitan Nonattainment Area was prepared by several state and regional organizations. The Regional Air Quality Council (RAQC) is "primarily responsible for identifying, analyzing and recommending control measures to include in the plan" (SIP 1995, I-1). The Colorado Department of Health, Air Pollution Control Division (APCD) is "responsible for developing, administering and enforcing air quality control programs adopted by the [State of Colorado] Air Quality Control Commission, including state implementation plans" (ibid).

Additional input to the SIP was provided by the Denver Regional Council of Governments (DRCOG), which "provides demographic and transportation data," and the U.S. Environmental Protection Agency, which is "responsible for reviewing and approving any implementation plan submitted by the State" (I-2).

## BOUNDARIES OF DENVER NONATTAINMENT AREA

A metropolitan nonattainment area is referred to by EPA as a Consolidated Metropolitan Statistical Area (CMSA). The Denver CMSA includes the counties of Denver, Jefferson, Boulder, Douglas, Arapahoe, and Adams in their entirety. However, the Air Quality Control Commission has excluded portions of Adams and Arapahoe counties east of Kiowa Creek as part of the Denver Metropolitan Nonattainment Area.

**Pollutants of Concern**

The SIP "addresses particulate matter with an aerodynamic diameter of less than or equal to a nominal 10 microns" (II-4). It also raises concerns for nitrogen oxides ($NO_X$) and sulfur dioxide ($SO_2$) as these secondary particles, emitted from stationary, mobile, and area sources, can make up "20-30 percent of elevated levels of $PM_{10}$ in the Denver area" (II-5).

## RELATIONSHIP OF PARTICULATE MATTER TO BROWN CLOUD

Another pollution problem that plagues the Denver area, the Brown Cloud, is closely associated with $PM_{10}$ (ibid). The sources for visibility impairment resulting from the Brown Cloud are the same as the sources of $PM_{10}$ but the sources contribute to each problem in different degrees. The example given in the SIP states that "while street sand and other sources of geologic dust make up more than 50 percent of $PM_{10}$ emissions, these sources are responsible for less than 15 percent of the Brown Cloud. Dust particles tend to be larger and contribute significantly to $PM_{10}$ mass but are not efficient at scattering light. On the other hand, tiny secondary particles are efficient scatterers of light and can make up 40 percent of the Brown Cloud" (ibid). This report will, therefore, focus on savings in health care expenditures related specifically to $PM_{10}$ in its cost-benefit analysis, and will not attempt to deal with benefits that may be accrued from improved visibility due to the reduction of Denver's Brown Cloud.

## OVERVIEW OF CONTROL MEASURES

The RAQC "selected a package of control strategies that focuses on reducing emissions from street sanding, wood burning, and industrial sources [...] to bring future emission levels to the point where the Denver metro area will be able to show attainment of the 24-hour $PM_{10}$ standard by the end of 1994 and maintenance of the standard through 1997" (V-1). In addition, contingency measures, to be adopted in the event of continued nonattainment, were included in a SIP revision attached to the SIP obtained from RAQC.

## WOOD BURNING CONTROL MEASURES

According to the RAQC, "[w]ood smoke from over 250,000 wood burning fireplaces and over 50,000 uncertified wood stoves constitute [sic] a major source of air pollution in the Denver metropolitan area. Wood smoke emissions can contribute up to 30 percent of elevated levels of fine particulate matter ($PM_{10}$), at least 25 percent of the Brown Cloud, and up to 10 percent of the carbon monoxide (CO) emissions, all significant pollution problems in the metro area" (VI-1). To combat these problems, three areas of wood burning control measures were addressed: 1) stringent certification standards for all new wood stoves and fireplace inserts; 2) reduced wood burning on days when meteorological conditions could lead to exceedances of air quality standards; and 3) cleaner-burning technology required by legislative mandate in new or remodeled construction (ibid). The specific elements of these control measures are:

- High pollution day wood burning restrictions
- Field surveillance
- Clean-burning technology requirements in new/remodeled construction
- Conversion of existing technology to cleaner-burning technology
- Prohibition of resale of used, uncertified wood stoves (VI-1-VI-8)

**Emission reductions:** The SIP predicts that high-pollution-day wood burning restrictions will reduce $PM_{10}$ emissions from fireplaces by 60 percent and emissions from wood stoves by 47.5 percent (VI-14). The SIP does not, however, make any predictions on $PM_{10}$ emission reductions from clean-burning technology, essentially natural gas appliances, or from the prohibition of resale on used, uncertified wood stoves. Therefore, the reduction in $PM_{10}$ emission rates from wood burning restrictions imposed during the winter months is 0.8 tons per day for wood stoves, and 1.4 tons per day for fireplaces, giving a total emission reduction of 2.2 tons per day.

While it is difficult to calculate reductions in terms of $PM_{10}$ *concentrations* based on the given information, an estimate of 50 percent reduction overall is not unlikely. This report will therefore use a rough figure of 4.2 $\mu g/m^3$ reduction in overall $PM_{10}$ due to wood burning restrictions.

**Economic impacts:** The SIP analyzes at length the economic impacts of its wood burning strategy, but nearly all of it deals with the costs and benefits associated with purchasing or converting to clean-burning technology, for which no emission reduction predictions are made. It can be extrapolated from data given throughout the SIP, however, that Denver area residents will reduce their wood fuel consumption in fireplaces by 29 percent, and wood stoves by 20 percent. This results in annual savings of $31.08 per fireplace, and $30.54 per uncertified wood stove. Using the figures quoted above of 250,000 fireplaces and 50,000 wood stoves in the Denver area results in annual cost savings of $9.3 million in wood fuel consumption. NOTE: While this figure will be used in subsequent cost analysis, it is obviously inflated by assuming 100 percent desire on the part of Denver area residents to burn wood during the winter, an assumption that is clearly without empirical evidence.

## STREET SANDING

The SIP states that "[e]missions of reentrained dust from street sanding and paved roads contribute significantly to elevated levels of $PM_{10}$ in the Denver metro area. Field studies and modeling efforts show that street sand and other geological material, principally from paved roads, make up from 40-50 percent of the $PM_{10}$ emissions inventory in the metro area. As a result, controlling street sand emissions can significantly reduce $PM_{10}$ levels in the Denver region" (VII-1).

The RAQC recommends a set of Street Sanding Guidelines intended to reduce the amount of sand applied for skid control by 20 percent in the City and County of Denver, 30 percent on I-25, and 50 percent in the Denver Central Business Area (CBA) (VII-10).

**Emission reductions:** The SIP predicts overall reduced emissions of 32 percent from the above reductions in street sanding, and an additional 10.8 percent reduction in paved road dust emissions from enhanced street sweeping activities, for a total reduction of 42.8 percent in reentrained dust in the atmosphere. This will result in a reduction from the uncontrolled level of 29.3 $\mu g/m^3$.

**Economic impacts:** The Street Sanding Guidelines recommended in the SIP are expected to cost local municipalities a total of $4523 per year for additional testing of sand for quality and durability, and increased maintenance of sanding equipment. Alternative deicers are expected to cost $60,000 per year to maintain and operate, not including a $100,000 capital equipment cost. Enhanced street sweeping will cost the region $263,000 per year. However, the SIP predicts an annual saving of $396,976 in reduced sand purchased for street sanding. Taken together, a net *savings* of $69,453 per year is predicted.

## OTHER MOBILE AND STATIONARY SOURCE EMISSION REDUCTION MEASURES

The SIP also provides technical analysis of other mobile and stationary source emission reduction measures, such as tailpipe and fuel measures, enhanced vehicle inspection, transportation control measures, and wintertime switching from coal to natural gas by local electrical power plants, but none of these analyses include cost analysis. They will therefore not be included in this report.

## ALTERNATIVE PM$_{10}$ CONTINGENCY MEASURES

According to the SIP, "[c]ontingency measures must be implemented if EPA determines that an area has failed to attain the PM$_{10}$ standard by the statutory deadline" (1). Here, the SIP clearly depicts cost and effectiveness analyses, but does not go into detail as to how the cost and effectiveness measures were calculated.

## METHODS

In this section, all of the above analysis will be brought together into a single cost-effectiveness analysis. It is interesting that the SIP would go to such great lengths to predict emission reductions and economic impacts, yet never put the two together into a cost-effectiveness measure on some solutions, completely

ignore the economic impact of other solutions, and then blithely throw out cost
and effectiveness analysis on the contingency measures with little detail given as
to how the figures were determined. Be that as it may, however, the SIP is the
only source available for this type of analysis.

Each measure for which cost data was provided in the SIP is included in
the following table. The cost-effectiveness factor is determined simply by
dividing the effectiveness by the annual cost. A negative cost-effectiveness factor
indicates cost *savings* due to pollution control measures.

**Table 1:** Cost-Effectiveness Analysis of $PM_{10}$ Reduction Measures

| Measure | Effectiveness $\mu g/m^3$ Reduction | Annual Cost (Benefits) | Cost-Effectiveness Factor |
|---|---|---|---|
| Wood burning restrictions | 4.2 | ($9.3 million) | -0.45 |
| Reduced street sanding | 29.3 | ($0.07 million) | -418.60 |
| Vacuum sweeping of Central Business District (CBD) | 13.0 average in CBD | $0.1 million | 130.00 |
| Alternative deicers in central Denver area; 75% equivalent sand reduction | 7.9 average in central area | $0.3 million | 26.33 |
| Alternative deicers in central Denver area; 75% equivalent sand reduction; vacuum sweeping in CBD | 19.3 average in CBD | $0.4 million | 48.25 |
| Regionwide 50% equivalent sand reduction | 4.7 regionwide | $12.2 million | 0.39 |
| Transportation control measures | 1.7 | $8.0 million | 0.22 |
| Seasonal switch to natural gas at metro area power plants | 17.5 | $38.6 million [using high estimate] | 0.45 |

# RESULTS

According to this analysis, reduced street sanding in the Denver Metropolitan Nonattainment Area is by far the most cost-effective measure presented for consideration by the RAQC. With its enormously negative cost-effectiveness factor, it is a wonder Denver area citizens allow any sanding at all! What this analysis does not include, however, is the cost of damage to vehicles due to the lack of skid control on snow and ice.

The next most cost-effective measure is certainly restrictions on wood burning during high pollution periods. The slightly negative cost-effectiveness factor calculated for this measure makes it financially beneficial for area residents to obey restrictions on wood burning when invoked. As wood burning below 7000 feet in elevation is done mostly for aesthetic purposes in the Denver area, this restriction does not impose any real hardship on the community.

Schemes involving alternative deicing, greater reductions in sanding, and vacuum sweeping of sand in central Denver are the next most cost-effective measures. Finally, seasonal switching from coal to natural gas at area electrical power plants and regional transportation control measures are the least cost-effective measures according to this analysis.

# EVALUATION OF COST-EFFECTIVENESS ANALYSIS

Cost-effectiveness analysis should be tested to determine if cost-effectiveness was, in fact, the most appropriate technique to use in the analysis (Levin 1983, 138-140). The following set of questions and answers will be used to make this determination:

1. What is the decision framework?
   *The specific context in which the decisions were made is unclear. One can assume RAQC was trying to achieve fixed effectiveness, and chose least-cost measures, the aggregate of which could reach the effectiveness goal of attainment.*

2.  Which alternatives are evaluated?
   *Only those alternatives for which the SIP provided cost analysis could be evaluated. This means the exclusion of other mobile and stationary source measures that may actually greatly affect the cost-effectiveness analysis.*

3.  How are costs estimated?
   *With a great deal of uncertainty!*

4.  Are the costs evaluated according to who pays them?
   *No.*

5.  Are costs presented in an appropriate mode, given the nature of the decision context?
   *No. Some costs are direct, some are indirect. Little attention to consistency was given by RAQC to its cost analysis.*

6.  Is the criterion of effectiveness appropriate to the analysis?
   *Many benefits and costs of reduced $PM_{10}$ pollution are omitted from the SIP.*

7.  Are there different distributional effects of the alternatives across populations?
   *No, the effects would be equally distributed across populations.*

8.  Does the analysis of results meet the overall standards for assessing effectiveness?
   *The reliability of the conclusions reached in both the SIP and this analysis are not as high as one would really like.*

9.  Are the cost-effectiveness comparisons appropriate?
   *Given all of the assumptions required to make this cost-effectiveness analysis, the ranking of measures based on the cost-effectiveness factor is reasonable.*

10. How generalizable are the results to other settings?
   *Other nonattainment areas in the Colorado area would probably reach the same conclusions reached in the Denver Nonattainment Area.*

Such negative and vague answers to these questions may lead one to conclude that cost-effectiveness analysis is not an appropriate technique for an analysis of remedies to particulate matter pollution in the Denver metro area. While it is true that no definitive conclusions could be drawn from the cost analysis, that is not a reflection on the technique so much as it is a reflection on the quality of data presented in the SIP's cost analysis. Much of the data presented is based on assumptions that are highly questionable, and cost metrics are not used consistently throughout the SIP. If the results are to be compared, it is essential that the calculation approaches be consistent (Suhrbier 1983, 6). It is obvious that the RAQC used data from numerous different sources in compiling the SIP, and made no attempt to standardize metrics so that comparative studies such as this one could be undertaken.

This is not a condemnation of the RAQC, however. Cost analysis was obviously a minor component in what was required in the SIP by EPA, if it was required at all.

## CONCLUSIONS

Cost-effectiveness analysis by itself can be highly misleading. In this analysis, it is clear that reduced street sanding and restrictions on wood burning in the Denver area should not only reduce particulate matter pollution significantly, but also reduce the Brown Cloud and put money in our pockets at the same time. None of this has occurred, at least not so as to be noticed by the average citizen.

Especially in the case of wood burning restrictions, the SIP predicts significant reductions in pollution while also predicting huge financial benefits to area residents. The problem, however, is that wood burning really contributes only 5 percent of the total $PM_{10}$ emissions. So reductions of 60 percent from fireplaces and 47.5 percent from wood stoves due to wood burning bans amount to total $PM_{10}$ reductions of 2.5 percent. And because wood burning is not practiced by 100 percent of the community at any given time, the assumed savings in wood fuel due to these restrictions are simply never realized.

A better use of cost-effectiveness analysis could be made in the case of comparing strategies that are similar to one another, and have as their basis the same set of cost data. For instance, two of the measures in the Alternative $PM_{10}$ Contingency Measures are described as follows:

**Table 2:** Cost-Effectiveness Analysis of Alternative $PM_{10}$ Contingency Measures

| Measure | Effectiveness $\mu g/m^3$ Reduction | Annual Cost | Cost-Effectiveness Factor |
|---|---|---|---|
| Alternative deicers in central Denver area; 75% equivalent sand reduction | 7.9 average in central area | $0.3 million | 26.33 |
| Alternative deicers in central Denver area; 75% equivalent sand reduction; vacuum sweeping in Central Business District | 19.3 average in CBD | $0.4 million | 48.25 |

The decision framework required to choose one of these alternatives would be an excellent use of cost-effectiveness analysis. The effectiveness of both measures is presented in the same units, as are costs. This makes the cost-effectiveness factor a reliable indicator of which measure has the most impact for the money spent. The second alternative is more than twice as effective for only 25 percent more money. With these data, a decision maker could easily use one of the two approaches to cost-effectiveness: fixed budget or fixed effectiveness. If the City of Denver is willing to spend up to half a million dollars on reducing particulates in the downtown area, the second option may be a very good choice as it is so much more effective yet still within budget. On the other hand, if the City must reduce particulates by, say, $5.0 \mu g/m^3$, and spend as little money as possible doing it, the first alternative is the better choice. Unfortunately, the real world examples presented throughout the rest of the SIP are not so clearcut.

In comparing this analysis to the savings in health care expenditures predicted by Chestnut in *Dollars and Cents*, the results are even less clear. Because the two measures undertaken by RAQC for which the SIP provides cost analysis are purported to produce *negative* costs for area residents, the additional negative costs in health care expenditures predicted by Chestnut are simply compounded by the measures required to attain the federal standards for $PM_{10}$ on which those savings are based. In short, residents of the Denver Metropolitan Nonattainment Area should see negative costs, that is, benefits, of $23.3 million each year from restrictions on wood burning, reduced street sanding, and their attendant reduced health care expenditures.

If this is indeed the case, it is the best news the world of environmental activism has ever heard. Unfortunately it just doesn't ring true.

## CRITICAL THINKING DRILLS

1.   Discuss the pros and cons of using cost-effectiveness analysis in making environmental policy. Do you feel it is a valid methodology for appropriating funds to environmental causes?

2.   Reach your own conclusions as to the best approach for the Denver metropolitan region to take based on the cost-effectiveness analysis given above. When would you apply the "fixed budget" approach to cost-effectiveness analysis? When would you apply "fixed effectiveness?"

3.   Critique the conclusion of this essay, that the cost-effectiveness analysis used on measures taken to reduce particulate matter in Denver's atmosphere exaggerates the monetary benefits gained in clearing the air.

## RESEARCH FOR THE ADVENTUROUS

Research an example of cost-effectiveness analysis applied to an environmental issue in your region (they are not hard to find). Write a 600-word analysis of the appropriateness of cost-effectiveness analysis as used on that particular issue.

# REFERENCES

American Lung Association. March 1994. *"The Perils of Particulates."* New York.

American Lung Association. 1995. Press Release. New York.

Brewer, G. D. and deLeon, P. 1983. *The Foundations of Policy Analysis.* Pacific Grove, CA: Brooks/Cole Publishing Company.

Chestnut, L. G. 1995. "Dollars and Cents: The Economic and Health Benefits of Potential Particulate Matter Reductions in the United States." Boulder, CO: Hagler Bailly Consulting, Inc.

Levin, H. M. 1983. *Cost-Effectiveness: A Primer.* Beverly Hills, CA: Sage Publications.

SIP. 1995. *Colorado State Implementation Plan for Particulate Matter (PM$_{10}$) Denver Metropolitan Nonattainment Area Element*; Regional Air Quality Council and Colorado Department of Health, Air Pollution Control Division.

Suhrbier, J. H. 1983. "Case Studies of Cost-Effectiveness of Transportation Measures to Improve Air Quality." *Cost-Effectiveness of Air-Quality Control Measures and Impact of the Environmental Review Process.* Washington, D.C.: Transportation Research Board, National Research Council, National Academy of Sciences;

Weimer, D. L. and Vining, A. R. 1992. *Policy Analysis: Concepts and Practice*; 2nd edition. Englewood Cliffs, NJ: Prentice Hall.

# CONSIDERATION OF AN EXCISE TAX ON CARBON IN THE STATE OF COLORADO

*The environmentalist often must consider taxation as a method of reducing human impact on the environment. Here carbon, in the form of carbon dioxide, has been identified as the primary greenhouse gas contributor to global warming. It is a product of fossil fuel combustion, along with other pollutants that contribute to metropolitan Colorado's "brown cloud." Its production could be significantly decreased through the introduction of an excise on the consumption of carbon-producing fossil fuels with little impact on the State's economy. This would make Colorado a world leader in the response to global warming issues, and would at the same time reduce Colorado's own air pollution problems. The tax could be revenue neutral such that the State's gross domestic product would be unaffected, and loss of revenues from tourism and federal funding which is dependent on maintaining low levels of pollution, would be avoided. This paper describes at a high level how such a tax may be implemented in Colorado.*

## BACKGROUND

The decision makers in this case clearly are the State Legislature, and the electorate if the initiative should become a ballot issue. Politically, an excise tax on carbon should be generally favored by the public, if studies done in other parts of the world are good indicators. In Japan, for example, 49% of the 10,000 residents interviewed responded favorably to a carbon tax, with 44% responding unfavorably (do Rosario 1992, 52). In the environmentally conscious State of Colorado, these numbers may well be more favorable. The fossil fuel industry is rightfully becoming increasingly concerned that U.S. government(s) may levy an excise on carbon (Crow 1991, 31). It is safe to assume industry will campaign against any carbon tax initiatives.

The economic issues that must be taken into consideration are the nature, structure, and level of an excise on carbon, and its macroeconomic effect on the State of Colorado. These concerns are addressed in more detail below.

An excise on carbon has two objectives:

- Decrease Colorado's greenhouse gas (GHG) contribution to global warming
- Decrease Brown Cloud pollutants

The tax must be imposed on carbon emissions, not on energy consumption in general (Cnossen & Vollebergh 1992, 29). In this way fossil fuel combustion is decreased, and non-fossil fuel sources of energy, such as hydroelectric, solar, and wind, are not penalized. It must be specifically expressed as a fixed amount per ton of carbon emitted, as opposed to an ad valorem percentage of fuel prices, to achieve the goal of reduced carbon emissions (ibid). The tax internalizes the cost of global warming and regional air pollution. Its success depends on the demand elasticity for fossil fuels, which has been shown to be high in other countries (Sterner et al 1992, 118), and can be expected to be equally high in Colorado, as consumers reduce consumption and eventually convert to cleaner fossil fuels or non-fossil fuel sources of energy.

An excise on carbon should be structured such that it is the carbon content of a fuel that is taxed. Thus, coal, which can have a very high carbon content, would be more costly to burn than petroleum, which would be more costly to burn than natural gas, the "cleanest" of the fossil fuels. Differentiating the excise by carbon content induces consumers to substitute cleaner fossil fuels for dirtier fuels, and non-fossil fuels for fossil fuels in general (Cnossen & Vollebergh 1992, 30). Eventually the State may want to consider a tiered fuel excise that would include a carbon excise, a sulfur excise (sulfur dioxide is a product of coal combustion, and is the primary contributor to acid rain), and a road use charge that internalizes the cost of infrastructure maintenance (ibid).

The level of the tax is obviously critical to achieving the stated objectives, based on the level of demand elasticity found in Colorado. One study in Great Britain suggests that initial levels could be raised by the ton oil equivalent of $3 per barrel, increasing to $10 per barrel by the year 2000 (Barker et al 1993, 298).

Another study suggests that prices in the U.S. may have to increase by the ton oil equivalent of $22 per barrel (Cnossen & Vollebergh 1992, 31). The level of the tax would require further study specific to the State of Colorado.

Effects on the Colorado economy would differ depending on how the tax is implemented. The tax should be revenue neutral if no effect on the State's economy is desired (Barker et al 1993, 296). In this way, the increased revenues from a carbon excise would go to the reduction of other state taxes, such as income tax, motor vehicle tax, or sales tax. A revenue neutral excise would be progressive, as fossil fuels have been shown to display high income elasticity (Sterner et al 1992, 118), and could be used to reduce regressive taxation such as the State sales tax. If the State desires to invest in non-fossil fuel development, excise revenues could be used for this purpose, but with the caveat that it may lead to a macroeconomic imbalance and possible inflation within the State's economy (ibid).

Reductions in GHGs and other fossil fuel pollutants could be substantial as consumers reduce their consumption through conservation, conversion to cleaner forms of energy, and increasing mass transit ridership. Electrical utilities would be encouraged to switch from coal, a major source of carbon as well as the pollutants that make up the brown cloud, to natural gas. This will avoid possible future loss of revenues from tourism, which could fall as Colorado becomes known for its air pollution problems, and will avoid loss of federal funding based on air quality in the State. Other flanking measures that could be accrued by the State include increased revenues from sales tax and motor vehicle taxes as consumers purchase new low fuel consumption vehicles in an effort to decrease their consumption of gasoline. Effects of the tax could be measured in reduced consumption of fossil fuels, fewer "Red Air Quality" days in the metropolitan Front Range region of Colorado, and lower levels of pollutants found in the Environmental Protection Agency's statistical sampling of the Colorado atmosphere.

## RECOMMENDATION

The State of Colorado should consider a carbon excise, as raising energy taxes is the single most effective tool in decreasing carbon emissions and other fossil fuel pollutants (Dower 1993, 2265). The tax would have little or no effect on the overall Colorado economy, and would increase the quality of life in

Colorado through cleaner air. Reduced fossil fuel emissions could go a long way toward keeping Colorado colorful -- not brown.

## CRITICAL THINKING DRILLS

1.   Should people pay for the damage they do to the environment as part of the cost of their own consumption? Defend your argument.

2.   How would a tax on carbon emissions serve to lower carbon emissions in the State of Colorado? Discuss "price elasticity" relative to consumption that leads to the emission of carbon in the United States. At what level do you think people will begin to reduce their consumption of fossil fuels? Could this reduction be achieved without increased taxes? How?

3.   Reduction of Denver's Brown Cloud is an indirect product of reduced carbon emissions that would result in better visibility in the region, especially during the winter when tourists are in town for local skiing. How can society put a price tag on the aesthetic value of clean air?

## RESEARCH FOR THE ADVENTUROUS

Research the concept of economic "externalities" and write a 600-word critique of its use in discussing environmental issues.

## REFERENCES

Barker, T., Baylis, S., and Madsen, P. 1993. "A UK Carbon/Energy Tax." *Energy Policy.* v 21. n 3.

Cnossen, S. and Vollebergh, H. 1992. "Toward a Global Excise on Carbon." *National Tax Journal.* v 45. n 1.

Crow, P. 1991. "Carbon Tax Concerns." *Oil and Gas Journal.* v 89. n 50.

do Rosario, L. 1992. "Burning Issue." *Far Eastern Economic Review.* v 155. n 34.

Dower, R. C. 1993. "The Right Climate for OECD Carbon Taxes?" *Environmental Science &Technology.* v 27. n 12.

Sterner, T., Dahl, C., and Franzen M. 1992. "Gasoline Tax Policy, Carbon Emissions and the Global Environment." *Journal of Transport Economics and Policy.* v 26. n 2.

# THE WIND

*The environmentalist must convince the rest of the world's people to modify their behavior so as to produce less pollution. In this whimsical idea for a clean car campaign aimed at young people, a fictitious automobile manufacturer has just produced a new car, called The Wind, that produces less pollution, but has poor acceleration and a top speed of 50 miles per hour. The company would like to aim its marketing at the young, first-time buyer market segment. The campaign will feature the slogan: Green is good.*

Scene: Two young guys in traffic on their way to the beach in Southern California. The driver is a proud new owner of The Wind, a small, low-emissions car.

Passenger: "Hey, new car, huh?"

Driver: "Yeah, it's called The Wind. It's practically smog-free."

Passenger: "How's the acceleration?"

Driver: "Well, it's gettin' us to the beach, isn't it?"

Passenger: "Sure, but the speedometer only goes up to 50 doesn't it?"

Driver: "Yeah, and the traffic is moving at about 23 miles an hour. How fast do you want to go? The difference is, everyone else out here is sitting in a smog factory, and we're hardly producing any smog at all."

Passenger: "Cool! Does it have air conditioning?"

Driver: "No way! That would just add weight and place more drag on the engine, not to mention all the CFCs that could escape and add to the ozone depletion. Besides, with the windows down you can smell the ocean breeze better!"

Passenger: "Excellent!"

Scene: The two guys jump out of The Wind at a beautiful, clean beach. Long shot of The Wind parked under palm trees, with the blue Pacific stretching out to the horizon.

Voice-over: "Ride The Wind. Because green is good."

## CRITICAL THINKING DRILLS

1.   Critique the theme of this fictitious advertising campaign: *Green is good.* Do you think it would sell environmentally friendly automobiles?

2.   How would you market an environmentally friendly vehicle, or any other product?

## RESEARCH FOR THE ADVENTUROUS

Study the advertising campaign of a product that is marketed as good for the environment. In 600 words, compare and contrast the campaign with a competitive product that is not marketed as being environmentally friendly.

# CONSIDER THIS

# U.S. DEPARTMENT OF ENERGY ALLOCATION
# OF RESEARCH AND DEVELOPMENT FUNDS

*The environmentalist must hold a vision of how environmental goals can be achieved, then propose the means by which society can achieve them. This essay outlines the budget requirements for achieving a solar-hydrogen economy in America within 20-25 years.*

*Energy serves as a symbol of what generally ails the economy and stimulates the drive to reach a new emotional consensus and political equilibrium* (Brewer & deLeon 1983, 185).

In times of great social evolution, advances in the sources and means the human race has relied upon for its energy requirements have historically led sociological advances. Steam power drove the Industrial Revolution, which was the basis for the great urbanization of Western society. Electricity, in only 200 years, fueled the Information Age, which has brought us to these times of knowledge at our fingertips -- and a far greater awareness of our impact and place on this planet Earth. In recent elections, the American public has voted for change. This budget describes, at a high level, how the Department of Energy should allocate funding to the research necessary to fuel the social goals of the American people.

Just as Congress wrestles with balancing the budget -- attempting to correct decades of deficit spending and federal debt -- our society must wean itself of its reliance on energy capital, and learn to rely solely on energy income. For our purposes, energy capital is the reserve of fossil fuels captured through photosynthesis in plants over millions of years and stored as petroleum and coal. Energy income, on the other hand, is the immediate capture of solar energy for current energy demands.

Reliance on energy income necessitates the formation of a solar/hydrogen economy. The research funding allocated through this budget proposal are meant to prepare America for such an economy over the next 20-25 years. To reach the goal of a solar/hydrogen economy within that time frame requires changes to our energy infrastructure and technologies but, more importantly, it requires changes in attitude and perception of what energy means to us and how we can best meet our needs.

## OVERVIEW

The research funding proposed here for the Department of Energy (DOE) represents several underlying theses: First, in most cases pure research should share funding with applied technology research. This is vitally necessary to our continued growth in the understanding of energy as a physical phenomenon. Second, funding should be aimed primarily at "the so-called soft path in energy that places little reliance on centralized authority" (184). This is in keeping with the American public's desire for individual autonomy using systems that are smaller and more responsive to the needs of a diverse society. Finally, there is emphasis placed on transportation and residential uses of energy, as these areas hold some of the greatest promise for application of the solar/hydrogen economy.

Research into *solar-powered hydrogen production* should be focused on transportation and residential applications. Hydrogen is especially attractive as fuel for transportation. According to Mark A. DeLuchi of the University of California at Davis and Joan M. Ogden at Princeton University, "It is the least polluting fuel that can be used in an internal combustion engine (ICE) and it is potentially available anywhere there is water and a clean source of power." Further, "[a] fuel cycle in which hydrogen is produced by solar electrolysis of water [...] would produce little or no local, regional or global pollution" (DeLuchi & Ogden 1993, 255).

The fuel-cell electric vehicle (FCEV) should be thoroughly researched. Peter Hoffmann, publisher of *The Hydrogen Letter*, has called the fuel cell the "back door into the hydrogen economy" (cited in Mayersohn 1993, 110-111). In this application, "a fuel cell converts chemical energy in hydrogen and oxygen directly into electrical energy" (DeLuchi & Ogden 1993, 256) to power an electric drive train.

Research further out on the horizon should include the development of a hydrogen/oxygen gas turbine to more efficiently transform the incredible potential in combusting hydrogen and oxygen into vehicular motion without intermediary transformation into electricity, and its inevitable energy losses due to the Second Law of Thermodynamics.

And on the more immediate front, the Department should fund research into the hydrogen enrichment of gasoline, in which initial studies have found reductions in nitrogen oxide pollutants of 30 to 40 percent (Mayersohn 1993, 70).

Research into residential applications of solar/hydrogen production should include cooking and heating with hydrogen produced in situ at the place of residence using solar electrolysis and tap water.

Research on *photovoltaic cells* should concentrate on pure research into semiconductor media and, perhaps more importantly, also concentrate on applied research into uses for these materials. Uses such as photovoltaic roofing materials on buildings and photovoltaic body paneling on vehicles, possibly even photovoltaic paints, should be investigated thoroughly.

The storage of energy should be researched as well as the production. While Joseph P. Maceda of H Power Corp. has stated "The best hydrogen storage system is no storage system at all" (68), implying a need for the development of in situ production of hydrogen for current energy demands, it is certain that the storage of hydrogen will be required, if only for the short term. Hydrogen has traditionally been viewed as extremely bulky to store as a compressed gas because tanks could generally only be pressurized to about 3000 psi. Research into carbon-wrapped aluminum-lined cylinders pressurized to at least 8000 psi may eliminate the economic and engineering concerns with storing hydrogen in vehicles (DeLuchi & Ogden, 259).

Other forms of energy storage should also be researched. Electrochemical devices (batteries) still hold promise for certain applications of stored electricity, while electromechanical devices (flywheels) have only recently been considered as a viable means for storing energy. What we must remember in researching storage devices is that we care only for storing *energy*, not limiting ourselves to storing electricity. I hope the distinction is clear.

Finally, pure research into *nuclear fusion* should be funded. This research is fundamental to our understanding of energy as a phenomenon, our understanding of the sun and the stars, indeed, our understanding of the universe and life itself.

## JUSTIFICATION

The justification for research into *solar/hydrogen production, photovoltaic cells, energy storage, and nuclear fusion* is not difficult based on abundance of resources, environmental concerns, and safety. The abundance of sunlight, water, and sand are obvious. The low-impact and even zero-impact environmental aspects of these technologies are certainly worth investigating in a world beset with air pollution, possible global warming due to greenhouse gases, and the as-yet unknown effects of continued ozone depletion in the upper atmosphere. And public safety is of utmost concern. While hydrogen has a reputation as an unsafe fuel (we've all seen the dramatic and horrifying pictures of the Hindenburg and Challenger tragedies), research has shown that "the hazards of hydrogen are different from, but not necessarily greater than, those presented by current petroleum fuels" (267).

## CONCLUSION

William Hoagland at the National Renewable Energy Laboratory in Golden, Colorado, has estimated America's conversion to hydrogen technology will take "20 to 25 years, to allow the infrastructure to be put in place" (Mayersohn 1993, 111). This proposed research budget could begin the arduous task of ensuring that America is ready for the solar/hydrogen economy within that time frame.

Hoagland has said, "The whole driver has changed. Once you bring in the environmental factor, there's really no equal to hydrogen" (ibid).

Energy from sunlight, water, and sand. Not alchemistry -- simply elegant chemistry.

## CRITICAL THINKING DRILLS

1. Is a solar/hydrogen economy the only way we can sustain life and civilization solely on energy income from the sun? Think of other ways solar energy might be indirectly tapped to lessen our dependence on energy capital. What impact(s) might these other means of capturing energy have on the environment?

2. Research the safety aspects of hydrogen as a fuel. How would you explain the dangers of hydrogen to a layperson? Would you say hydrogen is more dangerous than natural gas? Propane? Gasoline? What properties make a fuel dangerous? What properties make a fuel convenient?

3. Write a critique of this statement made by Joseph P. Maceda of H Power Corp., "The best hydrogen storage system is no storage system at all."

## RESEARCH FOR THE ADVENTUROUS

Read three articles on the use of hydrogen as a fuel and review them as if you were an editor for *The Hydrogen Journal.*

## REFERENCES

Brewer, G. D. and deLeon P. 1983. *The Foundations of Policy Analysis.* Pacific Grove, CA: Brooks/Cole Publishing Co.

DeLuchi, M. A. and Ogden, J. M. 1993. "Solar-Hydrogen Fuel-Cell Vehicles." *Transportation Research, Part A: General.* v 27. n 3.

Mayersohn, N. S. 1993. "The Outlook for Hydrogen." *Popular Science.* v 243. n 4.

# TOO LATE

*The environmentalist is often called upon to explain human behavior that is detrimental to the environment and, ultimately, detrimental to humans themselves. Here, on the popular (and fictitious) TV talk show Too Late, with host Greg Kinnear VII, a visitor from the 20th Century discusses the mindset of his contemporaries, and their attitudes toward natural resources.*

**Kinnear:** "Good evening, ladies and gentlemen. Tonight on *Too Late*, we're talking to Doug Joyce, a visitor from the 20th Century. Tell me, Doug, how could the people of your century feel justified in using up so much of the world's non-renewable resources such as oil and coal?"

**Joyce:** "Well, first of all, Greg, you're giving a little too much credit when you say we felt justified. That would imply that we *thought* about it, and had rationally decided to pursue the depletion of resources because our goals at the time warranted it. The fact is, most people simply didn't think about it at all. Remember, this was a time of great nation building, the apex of capitalism. It was also a time of bitter ethnocentricity, resulting in numerous wars that were very wasteful of resources, natural and human, and also a time of sublime egocentricity. We were the *me* generation, Greg, and the *me* generation doesn't worry about *you*."

**Kinnear:** "Ouch! ... So just what were the attitudes of your contemporaries toward natural resources?"

**Joyce:** "There were several features of our attitude worth mentioning: First, energy had, just before the turn of the century, suddenly become very easy to obtain. Whereas before about the 1880s, staying warm all winter may have meant days and days of chopping wood, we in the 20th Century simply set the thermostat. It automatically regulated the temperature of our homes and workplaces with no personal intervention. The utility company would then automatically bill us for the natural gas and electricity, and our bank accounts would automatically pay the bill. It was a 'no brainer,' Greg. We thought nothing of traveling across town or across the nation because all we had to do was put the nozzle in our gas tank, and put a credit card in the pump. There was no connection between the work derived from our use of natural resources, and the energy required in the formation of those resources.

"Second, we were consistently lied to by the big money interests so idolized by capitalism. We were told that solar energy could never be as effective as fossil fuels by the same petroleum companies that owned all of the patents to solar technologies. We were told that the new oil reserves in Alaska would see us through. We were told to 'take another look at plastic' because it was so readily recyclable, when in fact only 2% of the plastic that we consumed was actually being recycled. We were told that insignificant gains in automobile fuel efficiency were great advances in design, and that wholesale conversion to other forms of power would not be cost effective.

"And we believed them. We believed the lies because, as individuals, we generally did not have the educational background to discern that they were lies. Few of us could articulate the process of fossil fuel formation, in which the solar energy of millions of years of photosynthesis had been partially decomposed under incredible pressures, and millions more years, just so we could drive to the 7-11 for a Super Big Gulp. We just didn't really believe the First Law of Thermodynamics, which states that energy is neither created nor destroyed -- we thought we were creating energy ourselves just by paying for it! We thought the energy losses inherent in the Second Law of Thermodynamics, which says entropy is increasing, as we transformed fossil fuels from potential energy to heat energy to mechanical energy to electrical energy, were acceptable losses as long as we could afford to pay for them.

"We always figured that if the shit really hit the fan, and our easy supply of energy suddenly became *unaffordable*, somebody would somehow come up with some good ol' Yankee ingenuity, and invent a new way to create energy. We were not only egocentric, but highly egotistical as well.

"Finally, most people in the 20th Century refused to really think about their place in the universe. We kept our nose to the grindstone in meaningless jobs to divert our attention away from the really big questions like, 'Why am I here?' and 'What is my role in evolution?' In this way, we did not have to justify our use of natural resources, Greg. We did not have to consider our use of solar capital rather than solar income. We did not have to think."

**Kinnear:** "Well, thank you, Doug -- our time is about up. It's *Too Late*, and I am Greg Kinnear VII. We'll be right back after this announcement from Promethean Electric: 'Harnessing the sun, so *you* don't have to.' "

## CRITICAL THINKING DRILLS

1. Critique Joyce's assessment of people's unthinking consumerism of the 20th Century. Do you believe people consider their consumption habits? Explain your answer.

2. How does commercial advertising affect consumer habits in the U.S.?

## RESEARCH FOR THE ADVENTUROUS

Choose an advertising slogan from a current marketing campaign. Describe in 600 words how the slogan encourages people to either think about their consumption or not think about their consumption. A recent example might be "Get your own bag," but there are many to choose from.

# STANDING TO SUE: A STUDY OF ITS EVOLUTION THROUGH CASE LAW AND THEORY

*The environmentalist is often frustrated by the barriers encountered when attempting to use the judicial system to right environmental wrongs. One of the most important barriers to the "judicial activism" decried by so-called conservative critics, is that of standing to sue (Wenner 1994, 150). This essay looks at the concept of standing from a historical perspective, emphasizing environmental law cases illustrative of its evolution.*

## INTRODUCTION

Standing is a barometer of social conscience. It is a unique component of justiciability, the ability of the judicial system to try a particular case, in that it focuses on the litigant rather than the issue presented before the court (Reese 1995, 563). As such, it offers a powerful ticket of admission to those who *have standing*, but also imposes an equally formidable barrier to those who *have no standing*. But standing is not a static concept. Standing is a dynamic reflection of the society in which it operates and, as such it expands through "punctuated equilibria" -- long periods of unchanging equilibrium punctuated by episodes of dramatic change. These episodes are often concurrent with expansions in social awareness so important they are given names: the Industrial Revolution; the Civil Rights Movement; the Environmental Movement. *Legal standing is the Court's affirmation of the expansion of social conscience.*

This essay will first define standing as a legal concept, and will look briefly at the evolution of standing prior to the early environmental movement of the 1960s. Next it will focus on the liberalization of standing that took place in the Supreme Court during the Justice Douglas years of environmental law decisions. The antithetical backlash of decisions written by Justice Scalia will be detailed, with attention given to the Court's use of certiorari to make clear the conservative retreat from its previously liberalized concept of standing. Finally, a synthesis of standing as it applies to the rights of the unborn inhabitants of Planet Earth will be argued, with conclusions and implications for the future of environmental policy.

## DEFINITIONS OF STANDING TO SUE

**Standing - the legal right of a person or group to challenge in a judicial forum the conduct of another, especially with respect to governmental conduct (Gifis 1991, 460-461).**

This dictionary definition of standing tells us what the term *means*, but does little to inform us of who or what groups will be seen by the Court as having standing. In the United States, the term points back to Article III of the U.S. Constitution, in which "[t]he judicial Power shall extend to all Cases, in Law and Equity, arising under this Constitution, the Laws of the United States, and Treaties made, or which shall be made, under their Authority" (Vile 1993, 80). Article III speaks specifically to Controversies -- cases subject to judicial resolution -- and Parties -- those persons with a clear stake in the outcome of the case, but it still leaves a great deal of room for judicial discretion. As Chief Justice Warren wrote in *Flast v. Cohen* (1968), "Standing has been called one of the most amorphous concepts in the entire domain of public law." Its indeterminate nature would again be disparaged two years later in *Association of Data Processing Service Organizations, Inc. v. Camp*, when Justice Douglas wrote, "Generalizations about standing to sue are largely worthless as such."

The concept of standing to sue is not a litmus test in which, once a definition is committed to memory, the standing of every litigant appearing before a court of law can be immediately and inarguably determined. One's definition of standing depends a great deal upon which side of the bench one is situated. Noting Gifis' dictionary definition of standing, above, in which standing is defined in terms of "legal rights," one gets the impression of an open door to the bench as seen through the eyes of the Court. Compare that image to the following definition offered in a textbook on environmental law and policy:

*The standing doctrine limits the access of individuals and groups to judicial review and often frustrates attempts by citizens and organizations to prevent or preclude environmental law violations (Valente & Valente 1995, 36).*

Here, standing is seen as a barrier from the perspective of environmental activists attempting to gain access to the judiciary. When viewed from this perspective, standing to sue is definitely a closed door.

## THE EARLY EVOLUTION OF STANDING

So far, the concept of standing has only been expressed in terms of a *person*, which Gifis defines as "an individual or incorporated group having certain legal rights and responsibilities" (Gifis 1991, 350). But, in terms of standing to sue, the idea of a *person* becomes amorphous indeed. Article III mentions Citizens, States, and Subjects, but standing has been granted to a much broader set of Parties than those terms would imply. As Christopher Stone writes, "The world of the lawyer is peopled with inanimate right-holders: trusts, corporations, joint ventures, municipalities, Subchapter R partnerships, and nation-states, to mention just a few" (Stone 1974, 5). At the same time, standing has been denied to persons who would seem to readily fall into one or more of those groups denoted in the Constitution: blacks, Chinese, and women, for example.

Possibly the greatest leap of judicial faith was taken in 1809, when "[t]hat invisible, intangible and artificial being, that mere legal entity," the *corporation*, was granted standing in *Bank of the United States v. Deveaux*. This is even more astounding when one considers that nearly 50 years later, the Supreme Court would still deny standing to blacks as "a subordinate and inferior class of beings" in *Dred Scott v. Sandford*.

But is it really so astounding? After all, the nature of the U.S. judicial system is one in which remedy is often had in strictly financial terms. This being the case, a legal entity that exists for strictly financial reasons, such as a corporation, is far more likely to be seen as having a justiciable case involving the adverse economic affects of another's actions and a specific financial remedy. Groups such as blacks, women, environmentalists, etc. always want to approach the bench with problems that are not easily remedied with monetary awards. The

Court may address only those issues it can solve, so it simply disallows the presence of groups trying to bring "impossible" problems before it.

The fact that entities such as corporations are unable to speak for themselves does not disturb the Court, as lawyers have long represented clients unable to speak for themselves. The dumb, the comatose, and the dead have rightly been able to pursue their interests in court when they have had a justiciable case, so the extension of standing to an idea such as a corporation retaining legal counsel is not at all problematic.

## THESIS: THE LIBERALIZATION OF STANDING

A great example of punctuated equilibrium in the evolution of the concept of standing occurred in the early 1970s. It began with Justice William O. Douglas' dissent in *Sierra Club v. Morton* (1972), became reality in *United States v. SCRAP* (1973), and was reaffirmed in *Japan Whaling Association v. American Cetacean Society* (1986). These three cases represent a great liberalization in standing to sue as it applied to groups approaching the Court with environmental issues.

But any liberalization of standing to sue is merely the Court's reflection of expansions in the social conscience occurring outside the courtroom. Before describing the above cases, some background must be given on events in the history of environmental law and policy that immediately preceded those cases.

On January 1, 1970, the National Environmental Policy Act (NEPA) went into effect. In addition to legislative mandates that eventuated in the organization of the Environmental Protection Agency, this act contained language that environmental groups found they could use to their legal advantage in preventing further harm to the environment.

NEPA asserted as national policy that the federal government must "use all practical means ... to create and maintain conditions in which man and nature can exist in productive harmony" (Valente & Valente 1995, 54). And while it contained no specifications for the regulation of pollutants, as would later legislation, it did specifically mandate the performance of an environmental assessment (EA) prior to any action undertaken by the federal government and the publishing of an environmental impact statement (EIS) before taking any federal action that would significantly affect the environment (55). Special interest groups with any kind of an environmental bent were not slow to see the potential opportunity for litigation if only they could gain entrance to a court willing to hear their cases.

Not long after NEPA, Christopher Stone, a law professor at the University of Southern California, learned of an upcoming Supreme Court case in which the Sierra Club was attempting to sue the Forest Service for violation of its own regulations, and saw an opportunity to influence the Court's perception of environmental organizations and their standing to sue. Stone wrote the milestone article titled "Should Trees Have Standing? Toward Legal Rights for Natural Objects" in full knowledge that its publication in the *Southern California Law Review* would not occur in time for the Supreme Court justices to read it before deciding *Sierra Club v. Morton*. However, the one justice, William O. Douglas, most likely to be swayed by such an article was scheduled to write the journal's next "Preface to the Symposium on Law and Technology" and would be supplied with a draft of "Should Trees Have Standing?" several months before the Court would decide *Sierra Club* (Hardin 1974, xiv). Stone put the article together "at a pace that, as such academic writings go, was almost breakneck," (ibid) and, as the dissent given by Justice Douglas would later reveal, was instrumental in motivating the great liberalization of standing that was so soon to occur.

The Sierra Club filed suit as an organization with "a special interest in the conservation and sound maintenance of the national parks" (Sierra Club v. Morton 1972). The Court found, however, that it had failed to show that it or its members had been adversely affected by the actions of the Forest Service. Had Sierra Club won, wrote Garrett Hardin, author of "The Tragedy of the Commons," it "would no doubt have been called a 'watershed decision.' A watershed -- the topographical image must be kept in mind -- is ordinarily recognized only after one has passed over the ridge and is ambling down the other side" (Hardin 1974, xvi). But, though environmentalists were not yet "over the ridge" in terms of gaining standing to sue, the case proved to be a milestone for the dissent written and filed by Justice Douglas, in which he was joined by his long-time opponent, Justice Blackmun.

In his now-famous dissent, Justice Douglas referred directly to Stone's article when he wrote:

*The critical question of "standing" would be simplified and also put neatly in focus if we fashioned a federal rule that allowed environmental issues to be litigated before federal agencies or federal courts in the name of the inanimate*

*object about to be dispoiled, defaced, or invaded by roads and bulldozers and
where injury is the subject of public outrage. Contemporary public concern for
protecting nature's ecological equilibrium should lead to the conferral of
standing upon environmental objects to sue for their own preservation. [. . .]*

*Inanimate objects are sometimes parties in litigation. A ship has a legal
personality, a fiction found useful for maritime purposes. The corporation sole --
a creature of ecclesiastical law -- is an acceptable adversary and large fortunes
ride on its cases. The ordinary corporation is a "person" for purposes of the
adjudicatory processes, whether it represents proprietary, spiritual, aesthetic, or
charitable causes.*

*So it should be as respects valleys, alpine meadows, rivers, lakes, estuaries,
beaches, ridges, groves of trees, swampland, or even air that feels the destructive
pressures of modern technology and modern life. The river, for example, is the
living symbol of all the life it sustains or nourishes -- fish, aquatic insects, water
ouzels, otter, fisher, deer, elk, bear, and all other animals, including man, who
are dependent on it or who enjoy it for its sight, its sound, or its life. The river as
plaintiff speaks for the ecological unit of life that is part of it. Those people who
have a meaningful relation to that body of water -- whether it be a fisherman, a
canoeist, a zoologist, or a logger -- must be able to speak for the values which
the river represents and which are threatened with destruction (Sierra Club v.
Morton).*

Any reader with the good fortune of historical hindsight can readily see how
the prescient words of Justice Douglas would shortly come to fruition in
questions of standing for environmental organizations. One year later, a group of
law students calling themselves SCRAP (Students Challenging Regulatory
Agency Procedures) would take the lessons learned in *Sierra Club*, and combine
them with the NEPA requirement for an EIS in every major federal agency
action to win standing before the Supreme Court as a special interest group
litigating an environmental issue.

In *United States v. SCRAP* the plaintiffs argued that an order by the Interstate
Commerce Commission (ICC) allowing railroads to collect a surcharge on
freight rates would have an adverse affect on the recycling of products, and had
been promulgated without the publication of an environmental impact statement.
SCRAP, though it existed solely for the purpose of filing this suit, was granted
standing for two reasons:

1) SCRAP was "careful to plead" economic, recreational, and aesthetic harm to each of its members due to the adverse environmental impact of the ICC's rule.
2) SCRAP identified NEPA as the "relevant statute" that would support the group's standing in court when taken in conjunction with §702 of the federal Administrative Procedure Act (APA) (United States v. SCRAP).

Thus an environmental organization won standing to sue through careful attention to the requirements for standing as they were understood at the time.

In *Japan Whaling Association v. American Cetacean Society* the words of Justice Douglas were taken to their logical extreme when a whale watching organization successfully won standing to sue for the adverse affects it suffered from the continued harvesting of whales by Japanese whalers. The plaintiffs filed suit in federal district court asking for a mandate compelling the Secretary of Commerce as an absolute duty to certify to the President that Japan was harvesting whales in excess of quotas established by the International Whaling Commission (IWC). Recent Congressional activity would then require the President to impose economic sanctions upon Japan, including the prohibition of fish importation from the offending country. The Court found that whale watchers would indeed be adversely affected by Japan's excessive whale harvest, and this type of injury was found to pass the "zone of interests" test. The American Cetacean Society was granted standing to sue.

In retrospect, the years between *Sierra Club* and *Japan Whaling* are seen as the Golden Age of U.S. environmental awareness. The Clean Water Act (CWA), Toxic Substances Control Act (TSCA), Resource Conservation and Recovery Act (RCRA), and Comprehensive Environmental Response, Compensation, and Liability Act (CERCLA or Superfund) were all enacted in the wake of "Should Trees Have Standing?"

## ANTITHESIS: A CONSERVATIVE COURT'S HASTY RETREAT FROM THE LIBERALIZATION OF STANDING

Throughout the 12 years of the Republican administrations of Presidents Ronald Reagan and George Bush, Supreme Court appointments were made that created a Court decidedly more conservative than the Court that had liberalized standing to sue a decade earlier. The Court, in fact, took it upon itself to rein in the loose interpretation of standing bequeathed to it. This is seen in two cases involving environmental groups and the Department of Interior, and the legal maneuvering, known as a writ of certiorari, used by the Court to make its point.

In *Lujan v. National Wildlife Federation*, which has come to be known as Lujan I, an environmental organization filed suit against the Bureau of Land Management (BLM) challenging a "land withdrawal review program" recently initiated by the BLM. The National Wildlife Federation (NWF) alleged that its members' recreational and aesthetic enjoyment of land would be adversely affected by BLM's program. The U.S. District Court, District of Columbia, granted summary judgment, in which normal legal proceedings are disregarded in order to resolve the issue at hand in a timely fashion, against the NWF at the request of Secretary of the Interior, Manuel Lujan. The District Court of Appeals reversed and remanded, but the Supreme Court granted certiorari and reversed. Justice Blackmun dissented and filed, with Justices Brennan, Marshall, and Stevens joining (Lujan v. National Wildlife Federation).

The majority held that the NWF had no standing to sue for three reasons:

1) The affidavits filed by members of the NWF were insufficient to show that the affiant's interests were actually affected.
2) The BLM program was not an "agency action" or "final agency action" as defined by the federal APA.
3) Affidavits showing that the NWF's ability to fulfill its informational and advocacy functions was adversely affected failed to identify an agency action that was the source of the group's alleged injuries (ibid).

The holdings are not so significant in themselves as they are important precursors to the Court's findings two years later in a case that came to be known as Lujan II. Here we see the true intent of the Court in its effort to withhold standing from environmental groups attempting to sue the federal government as the "private attorney generals" predicted by the Court in *Sierra Club*.

In *Lujan v. Defenders of Wildlife* (Lujan II), a coalition of environmental organizations filed suit against the Secretary of the Interior, challenging a regulation requiring federal agencies to confer with the Secretary *only* with respect to federally funded projects in the U.S. and on the high seas. The U.S. District Court, District of Minnesota, dismissed the case for lack of standing, but the Eighth Circuit Court of Appeals reversed the decision on standing. The District Court then ruled in favor of the Defenders of Wildlife, and the Court of

Appeals affirmed. The Supreme Court *again* granted certiorari, and reversed and remanded the case on lack of standing, Justices Blackmun and O'Connor dissenting (Lujan v. Defenders of Wildlife).

It is here, in Lujan II, that Justice Scalia made clear the three-point test of standing now in use, especially in regards to environmental litigation:

1) There must be injury in fact.
2) There must be causal connection between the injury and a specific federal action.
3) It must be "likely," as opposed to "probable," that the injury will be redressed by a favorable decision (ibid).

The majority held that the Defenders of Wildlife failed the standing test on two of the three points: 1) the plaintiffs did not assert sufficiently imminent injury to have standing; and 2) their claimed injury was not redressable (ibid). In short, the Court would grant standing only to those able to show definite injury, usually of a financial nature, that could be directly linked to federal action, and could be financially remedied by the Court. Organizations attempting to sue on behalf of some vague notion of public good would not find a friendly ear in the current Court.

Of significance in these cases is the Court's use of the *writ of certiorari* in order to inspect the proceedings of lower courts and reverse their findings on the standing of environmental organizations. Justice Scalia and at least three other Justices in this conservative court thought the question of standing had gotten sufficiently out of hand to warrant exercising their discretionary use of certiorari, and step in to define a litmus test that, in fact, *could* be committed to memory and applied to any litigant appearing before a Constitutionally vested court. And this is the current state of the legal arts, especially as practiced in the United States.

Does it come as any surprise that the Reagan/Bush years are seen as such a low point in environmental activism?

Now, however, environmental issues are handled more and more on the international -- no -- planetary -- stage. As pollution and natural resource depletion tend to disregard state borders, so too must environmental law overlook national sovereignty if it is to be effective in combatting the environmental problems currently facing the inhabitants of Planet Earth.

## SYNTHESIS: THE STANDING OF FUTURE GENERATIONS

Christopher Stone and Justice Douglas tried to gain standing for inanimate objects, and were at least partially successful. Today the thrust of those pushing the envelope of standing to sue aims at protecting the rights of future generations, especially as those rights are related to the environment in which future generations will find themselves.

The notion of standing for the unborn is not without powerful motivation. The Preamble to the United States Constitution states:

*We the People of the United States, in Order to form a more perfect Union, establish Justice, insure domestic Tranquility, provide for the common defence, promote the general Welfare, and secure the Blessings of Liberty to ourselves and our Posterity, do ordain and establish this Constitution for the United States of America.*

It is clear from the phrase "ourselves and our Posterity" that the Founding Fathers intended to include future generations in the "People of the United States." Yet, the notion of future generations having standing to sue for protection from environmental harms inflicted by the current generation is completely untested, even though NEPA requires the U.S. "to fulfill the responsibilities of each generation as trustee of the environment for succeeding generations." We must look beyond the borders of the United States to find leading edge work on the issue of standing for future generations.

One case of interest comes out of the Philippines. There, in *Oposa v. Factoran*, popularly known as the "Children's Case," the Supreme Court of the Philippines granted standing in 1993 to a group of children suing the government to uphold their own environmental rights as well as the environmental rights of children as-yet unborn (Allen 1994, 713).

Until as recently as 25 years ago, 53% of the Philippine archipelago was covered by rainforest -- a total of 16 million hectares. Today only 2.8% of the nation's lands, less than 850,000 hectares, are in old-growth rainforest, though another 3 million hectares are in unusable secondary growth forest (714). These lands are under the regulation of the Philippine Department of the Environment and Natural Resources (DENR), whose organic legislation includes a mandate to protect terrestrial and marine environments "for present and future generations of Filipinos" (716). Yet, in 1990, the DENR granted timber leases totalling 3.89

million hectares -- *this in a country that had less than one million hectares of forest remaining!*

An environmental group known as PEN (Philippine Ecological Network), filed suit on behalf of 41 children against the Secretary of DENR. The suit sought a court order requiring DENR to cancel its existing timber leases and enjoin the agency from issuing additional timber leases. The Trial Court of Makati granted DENR's motion to dismiss, but the Children requested and were granted certiorari by the Supreme Court of the Philippines.

The plaintiffs argued that they and future generations have a right to a healthy environment, and cited Philippine environmental and administrative law, the national constitution, and natural law to support their claim. They cited *United States v. SCRAP* and *Sierra Club v. Morton* (Philippine law relies heavily on Anglo-American theories and precedents) in arguing for standing, demonstrating that they had passed the *SCRAP* test of "real and perceptible harm." Justice Hilario Davide, Jr., in granting standing to the Children wrote that "[b]y asserting their own right to a sound environment, the children were also fulfilling their responsibility to protect that right for future generations" (715-717). Planet Earth thus had its first successful test of standing to sue on behalf of future generations.

The implications of *Oposa* are profound. First, the foundation concept of environmental guardianship for future generations has been laid. Second, objections based on our inability to determine the interests of future generations have been dismissed by assuming interests similar to our own. Lastly, the tests required by Lujan II were overcome through the Children's demonstration of harm to themselves but, as Allen points out:

*Congress still could pass a statute recognizing that future generations have environmental rights and confering [sic] standing on those who seek to advocate their interests. To leave no doubt, Congress should clearly express this preference and provide guidance on the degree of causation required, what injuries may be compensated, and the rules for bringing such suits (736).*

Policy exists in formal language. The policy of the United States concerning the environmental rights of future generations is contained in the National Environmental Policy Act. But years of emphasis on economic development by a conservative Court have left us in need of further clarification from Congress.

# CONCLUSIONS

Decisions of the Court make tangible our social conscience. As such, the concept of standing to sue reflects our highest ideals of who has legal rights within our judicial system. When social conscience expands, standing becomes more inclusive. But does it not work the other way as well? Do not Christopher Stone, Justice Douglas, and the Philippine Children's Case demonstrate that expanded notions of standing can lead to greater social awareness of entities not normally represented in court? Trees. Rivers. Our unborn children. All have found standing, and all have subsequently gained greater attention from current society in light of that standing.

This may seem a slippery path, down which we will slide to potential absurdities such as standing to sue granted to representatives of the "Gaia hypothesis," the theoretical biological feedback system proposed by James Lovelock that keeps the Earth in global biogeochemical homeostasis (Smith 1992, 401). But when mankind assays to adversely affect the planet as a whole, as in, for example, the total destruction of old-growth forests or the incessant production of atmospheric greenhouse gases, *somebody* will have to sue on behalf of the planet: inanimate objects, current inhabitants, future generations, and all.

And the Court will grant standing when our conscience demands it.

# CRITICAL THINKING DRILLS

1. Find a recent court case (it need not be environmentally related) in which an organization has filed for standing to sue. What approach did the organization use in order to gain standing? Did it work? How might the organization have better stated its case?

2. Should trees have standing? If so, who should be entrusted with representing them in court? Can you think of some other non-human entities that should have standing but currently do not?

3. Consider the intergenerational argument. Do the unborn have rights? Are they the same rights that the living enjoy? How can these rights be upheld?

## RESEARCH FOR THE ADVENTUROUS

Read *Should Trees Have Standing?* by Christopher Stone, then read Justice Douglas' dissent in Sierra Club v. Morton. Write a 600-word summary of how Stone used an article in a legal journal to influence a Court's decision.

## REFERENCES

Allen, T. 1994. *"The Philippine Children's Case: Recognizing Legal Standing for Future Generations."* The Georgetown International Environmental Law. Washington, D.C.: Georgetown University.

Association of Data Processing Service Organizations, Inc. v. Camp. 1970. Supreme Court of the United States. 397 U.S. 150, 90 S.Ct. 827, 25 L.Ed.2d 184.

Bank of the United States v. Deveaux. 1809. 9 U.S. (5 Cranch) 61, 86.

Dred Scott v. Sandford. 1856. 60 U.S. (19 How.) 396, 404-05.

Flast v. Cohen. 1968. Supreme Court of the United States. 392 U.S. 83, 88 S.Ct. 1942, 20 L.Ed.2d 947

Gifis, S. H. 1991. *Law Dictionary.* Hauppauge, NY: Barron's Educational Series, Inc.

Hardin, G. 1974. "Foreword." Stone, C. D. *Should Trees Have Standing?* Los Altos, CA: William Kaufmann, Inc.

Lujan v. Defenders of Wildlife. 1992. Supreme Court of the United States. 112 S.Ct. 2130.

Lujan v. National Wildlife Federation. 1990. Supreme Court of the United States. 110 S.Ct. 3177.

Reese, J. H. 1995. *Administrative Law: Principles and Practice.* St. Paul, MN: West Publishing Co.

Sierra Club v. Morton. 1972. Supreme Court of the United States. 405 U.S. 727, 92 S.Ct. 1361, 31 L.Ed.2d 636.

Smith, R. L. 1992. *Elements of Ecology.* New York: HarperCollins Publishers, Inc.

Stone, C. D. 1974. *Should Trees Have Standing?* Los Altos, CA: William Kaufmann, Inc.

United States v. SCRAP. 1973. Supreme Court of the United States. 412 U.S. 669, 93 S.Ct. 2405, 37 L.Ed.2d 254

Valente, C. M. and Valente, W. D. 1995. *Introduction to Environmental Law and Policy*. St. Paul, MN: West Publishing Company.

Vile, J. R. 1993. *A Companion to the United States Constitution and Its Amendments*. Westport, CT:Praeger Publishers.

Wenner, L. M. 1994. "Environmental Policy in the Courts." Vig, N. J. and Kraft, M. E., eds.

*Environmental Policy in the 1990s*. Washington, D.C.: Congressional Quarterly, Inc.

# A DAY IN THE LIFE

*The environmentalist is told to think globally, act locally. There is no action more local than the personal decisions of consumption we make day in and day out. In this essay I look at my own consumption patterns. I think they're pretty good. But even so, it is simply mind-boggling how energy and resource intensive the American lifestyle can be.*

My involvement in the food web is more complex than a peatland bog. I choose my food based on a mix of environmental, economic, health, and spiritual reasonings. I eat only fruits, nuts, and cereals, leafy vegetables, and dairy products. I must always weigh the value of produce based on its proximate cultivation, and the methods used in its production: organic and pesticide-free, or conventional. I grow a good deal of my own food, which is about as proximate, organic, and pesticide-free as one can get. A sample of my diet follows, as recorded on Tuesday, November 28, 1995:

| Foodstuff | Origin | Reasons |
|-----------|--------|---------|
| SPIRU-TEIN food supplement | Melville, NY, USA | Health -- contains spirulina |
| Nonfat milk (1 cup, mixed w/ SPIRU-TEIN, above) | Boulder, CO, USA | Organic, no pesticides, no antibiotics, no hormones; proximate |
| Apple (1, Red Delicious) | Washington, USA | Organic |

| Rice (2 cups, Basmati) | Foothills of the Himalayas | Protein (completed by tofu) |
|---|---|---|
| Baked tofu | Boulder, CO, USA | Protein (completed by rice) |
| Pear (1, Bosc) | USA | Organic |
| Pesto bagel | Denver, CO, USA | Fiber |
| Cream cheese | USA | Flavor |
| Orange (1, Valencia) | Florida, USA | Organic |
| Corn chips (unsalted) | USA | Protein (completed by cheese) |
| Cheese (Monterey Jack) | USA | Protein |
| Caesar salad | USA | Fiber |
| Apple pie | USA | Snack |
| Water (1 gallon, filtered) | Rocky Mountains | Life |
| Coffee (2 mugs) | Who knows? Probably some converted rainforest in Colombia | Stimulant |

Well, ok, nobody's perfect... Obviously, even for one who *tries* to eat from proximate production, my diet traveled many thousands of miles to get to my table that day. Much of it is not "organic," as I would prefer, but at least some of it did as little damage to the environment (not to mention my own internal environment) as possible. About the best I can say is this: the absence of meat in my diet greatly reduces the negative externalities we face in water consumption, methane emissions, grazing issues, and all of the chemical and topsoil issues we face in growing enough grain to feed the animals we need to overfeed ourselves with meat. I defer to James Carse when he says:

*Gardeners slaughter no animals. They kill nothing. Fruits, seeds, vegetables, nuts, grains, grasses, roots, flowers, herbs, berries -- all are collected when they have ripened, and when their collection is in the interest of the garden's heightened and continued vitality. Harvesting respects a source, leaves it unexploited, suffers it to be as it is (Carse 1986, 151).*

As far as my non-dietary consumption is concerned: I drive a Honda Civic VX, which had the highest fuel mileage of any car sold in the U.S. when I purchased it, and my commute to work is only about two miles. Yet, even though I strictly adhere to the speed limit, my fuel consumption and carbon dioxide contribution were not zero, though they were undoubtedly far below the U.S. average. I reduce, reuse, and recycle, precycle and compost -- but I'm not kidding myself. I still contribute to the solid municipal waste problem. At this point, my epitaph could only read: "Hey, he tried..."

## CRITICAL THINKING DRILLS

1.  Consider your own diet in terms of the distance it travels to reach your plate. How could you reduce this distance? Do you feel it is worth the effort or expense to do so? Why?
2.  Critique the quote above by James Carse. Do you agree with his sentiments concerning harvesting? How would you apply his argument metaphorically to larger environmental issues?

## RESEARCH FOR THE ADVENTUROUS

Monitor your own consumption for one day. In 600 words, summarize and characterize your diet and other consumption patterns. Do you consider them to be worthy of an environmentalist? Do you even consider that to be a valid question?

## REFERENCES

Carse, J. P. 1986. *Finite and Infinite Games.* New York: Ballantine Books.

# WILDLIFE CONSERVATION

*The environmentalist should be aware of differences in opinion regarding the conservation of wildlife. What is wildlife conservation? Is it policy or philosophy? Public or personal?*

The single greatest conservation practice we could institute to protect wildlife is education. We must each be made more aware of our impact on the planet so that we can each make sustainable development decisions. Furthermore, we must make conservation economically attractive through the use of resource pricing that takes the future value of a commodity into account, and do away with subsidies that make unsustainable practices economically viable.

We must balance the needs of the human species with the needs of the planet as a whole. We *are* part of the planet! We must protect ecosystems such as rainforests and oceans and all of their inhabitants, and learn to place the highest value on old growth forests simply because they are old growth. John Mohawk expresses it well when he says, "What is needed is the liberation of all the things that support Life -- the air, the waters, the trees -- all the things which support the sacred web of Life" (Mohawk 1994, 169).

We must set aside whole tracts of land -- for ourselves and for the future. We must ensure the continued presence of interconnecting corridors between these tracts for the safe migration of plants and animals. We must end our reliance upon resource capital, and learn to live solely on the energy income we receive freely from the sun. We must stop mining and damming our water resources, which we turn right around and pollute immediately upon consumption. There is so much we can do -- so much that we must do. But in the end we *must* have the information we need for each of us to make our own sound sustainable development decisions. Aldo Leopold said it best:

*I have read many definitions of what is a conservationist, and written not a few myself, but I suspect that the best one is written not with a pen, but with an axe. It is a matter of what a man thinks about while chopping, or while deciding what to chop. A conservationist is one who is humbly aware that with each stroke he is writing his signature on the face of his land (Leopold 1949, 68).*

## CRITICAL THINKING DRILLS

1.   What is your definition of a conservationist? How does it differ from that of a preservationist? An environmentalist?

2.   Do you agree that education is the most important factor to improving the environment? If so, explain how education affects the environment. If not, what do you consider to be the single most important conservation practice?

## RESEARCH FOR THE ADVENTUROUS

Find some statistics describing the impact that greater education has on a society and its environment. Consider the changes to population growth, consumption, etc. and write a 600-word analysis of your findings.

## REFERENCES

Leopold, A. 1949. *A Sand County Almanac.* New York: Oxford University Press.

Mohawk, J. 1994. "The Great Law of Peace." Markate Daly, ed. *Communitarianism: A New Public Ethics.* Belmont, CA: Wadsworth, Inc.

# DEEP POLICY:
## CONSCIOUS EVOLUTION IN THE FOREST

*The environmentalist evolves with the ability of the human species to consciously adapt to life on planet Earth. Anthropocentric and individualistic foundations result in forest management policy based on linear, single-dimensional, marginal analysis detrimental to the wellbeing of the forest ecosystem. Recent theories from the fields of ethics, economics, and policy analysis find that nonlinear, multidimensional analysis is possible, provided one can divorce oneself from anthropocentric and individualistic tendencies. Deep policy is introduced as a policy perspective that encourages questioning the fundamental values upon which policy decisions are made, just as deep ecology encourages a similar questioning of ecological values. An experiment is proposed for forest management in the Pacific Northwest, in which a self-realizing Forest Board demonstrates punctuated equilibrium in forest management policy.*

## INTRODUCTION

The problems facing the manager of forest policy today are many and multidimensional due to the multidimensional uses and threats in the forest. This essay introduces the concept of *deep policy* for finding the basis of threats to the forest. To describe deep policy, it is necessary to conduct a descriptive analysis of the various ethical, economic, and policy theories upon which we base policy decisions. Deep policy predicts the accelerated evolution of policy in the management of forest resources -- periods of punctuated equilibrium in the lexicon of contemporary students of evolution.

First, a Thesis describes important theories from the studies of ethics, economics, and policy analysis to explain how we came to implement the policies in effect today, including specific application to policies of the U.S. Forest Service. Next, an Antithesis describes theories of how we *ought* to behave, and the policies we should implement to encourage that behavior. Finally, a Synthesis brings the two together, applying the techniques of deep policy to offer a solution to the problems of modern forest management: A prescription for the implementation of an experimental Forest Board governing forest in the Pacific Northwest, based loosely on a recent citizen initiative passed to amend the constitution in the State of Colorado.

# THESIS

Forest management policy in the United States is based primarily on the utilitarian tradition of 19th Century writers such as John Stuart Mill and Jeremy Bentham. This tradition may be summed up by the phrase "the greatest good for the greatest number" (des Jardins 1993, 29). "The greatest good" is a completely anthropocentric idea that has little to do with the desires or inherent worth of other species, ecosystems, or the environment. There is also no question as to the meaning of "the greatest number," for this refers solely to the greatest number of humans, harking back to the underlying theme of individualism upon which the utilitarian tradition is based. The utilitarian tradition is thus completely anthropocentric and individualistic. It looks only for *the greatest good for the greatest number of people.*

At first glance, it would appear as though John Rawls' *theory of justice*, which represents a major contribution to the philosophy of 20th Century western society, might apply equally to nonhuman as well as human beings. His "original position," from which participants in life would determine ethical fairness from behind a "veil of ignorance," implies no separation between nonhuman participants and human participants. However, when Rawls states his Two Principles of Justice, he clearly leaves no room for non-anthropocentric sentiment. He says:

*First: each person is to have an equal right to the most extensive basic liberty compatible with a similar liberty for others.*

*Second: social and economic inequalities are to be arranged so that they are both (a) reasonably expected to be to everyone's advantage, and (b) attached to positions and offices open to all (Rawls 1971, cited in Daly 1994, 77).*

Rawls admits that "[j]ustice as fairness is not a complete contract theory" (74). He realizes its anthropocentric nature when he states:

*Obviously if justice as fairness succeeds reasonably well, a next step would be to study the more general view suggested by the name "rightness as fairness." But even this wider theory fails to embrace all moral relationships, since it would seem to include only our relations with other persons and to leave out of account how we are to conduct ourselves toward animals and the rest of nature. I do not contend that the contract notion offers a way to approach these questions which are certainly of the first importance; and I shall have to put them aside (ibid.).*

Rawls advances the utilitarian mantra to one of "the greatest good for all people." However, philosopher Michael Sandel notes that the individual is still encouraged to achieve his own greatest good, and interprets Rawls such that, "Whereas society consists of a plurality of subjects and so requires justice, in private morality, utilitarianism seems to suffice; where others are not involved" (Sandel 1982, cited in Daly 1994, 85). And upon this foundation was built the neoclassical economic paradigm.

Contemporary studies of economics define the "dismal science" as a social science that models the use of scarce resources by consumers, producers, and government. These participants take action based on rational choice, a logical and predictable decision making method based on the individual goals of each participant.

To evaluate the utilities of consumers, producers, and government, we use marginal analysis, the basis of neoclassical economics. Within this paradigm, we portray the single-dimensional actions of consumers and producers as curves on x-y axes of quantity and price. We see supply as having a positive slope, such that the quantity of goods supplied by producers increases with price. We see demand as having a negative slope, such that the quantity of goods demanded by consumers decreases as the price goes up. When we apply marginal analysis to the goals of government, we see social utility maximized at the point where the difference between costs, which are increasing at an increasing rate, and benefits, increasing at a decreasing rate, is greatest. Furthermore, we see the curves produced by marginal analysis as smooth. There are no abrupt deviations in the rate of change to the curve when examined over an arbitrarily small section of the curve. It is no accident that the evolution of policy should appear smoothly incremental as well.

When government seeks to maximize social utility, it forces public administrators to make rational choices based upon knowledge of the present situation. It is thus irrational for the administrator to stray very far from knowledge of the present, compelling decisions that seem to "muddle through" the present situation, and rarely result in decisions that propel policy in radically new directions. G. D. Brewer and P. deLeon quote Charles E. Lindblom, one of public administration's most prominent writers, to explain:

*Setting goals or objectives is not easy. The inherent difficulty of defining policy objectives prompted Lindblom to expound upon the virtues of muddling through:*

*"As to whether the attempt to clarify objectives in advance of policy selection is more or less rational than the close intertwining of marginal evaluation and empirical analysis, the principal difference established is that for complex problems the first is impossible and irrelevant, and the second is both possible and relevant."*

*Lindblom's statement is more descriptive than prescriptive, although he presents a good argument for the marginalist approach (Brewer & deLeon 1983, 48-49).*

Compare this view of policy evolution to Charles Darwin's theories of natural selection and adaptation, on which we base our explanation of biological evolution. In the Darwinian view, species adapt to changing environmental conditions (the present situation) through constant yet minute variations (the muddling through of marginal analysis) in hereditary attributes. In policy science, policies incrementally advance through the six basic phases of initiation, estimation, selection, implementation, evaluation, and termination (17-18). Those attributes that enhance survival in the present situation are passed on to the next policy, and the transition from one policy to another is smooth and uninterrupted. Brewer & deLeon describe decision making as an ongoing process that cannot be isolated from its contextual setting, saying:

> *This school of thought particularly rejects the concept of the "economic man" as a decision maker in favor of the limited knowledge, bounded rationality, "incremental" concept of decision making, in which actions iteratively lead to decisions and policies (188).*

## APPLICATION TO U.S. FOREST SERVICE POLICY

The evolution of policy in the U.S. Forest Service (USFS) is very much a product of all of the above theories on how species, including the human species, react to changing conditions in the environment.

As an agency within the U.S. Department of Agriculture (USDA), the mission of the Forest Service has always been understood to "mean that the Forest Service was to harvest timber on the national forests in the manner that it thought best." The Forest Reserves Amendment of 1891 authorized the President of the United States to set aside forest reserves. Its Organic Act of 1897 set general guidelines for administering forestlands, and the turn-of-the-century "conservative" movement of Gifford Pinchot advocated silvicultural methods of timber management aimed at increased resource yields. Until recent decades the Forest Service has been granted "unfettered authority" in the administration of timber sales to private parties (Coggins et al 1993, 606-608).

Then in 1960, Congress passed the Multiple-Use, Sustained-Yield Act (MUSY) to mandate a broader range of uses within the national forests, and ensure that they would continue to yield for generations to come. MUSY names five forest resources thought at the time to be of paramount value: outdoor recreation, range, timber, watershed, and wildlife and fish. It defines *multiple use* as "[t]he management of all various renewable surface resources of the national forests so that they are utilized in the combination that will best meet the needs of the American people[.]" MUSY then defines *sustained yield* as "the achievement and maintenance in perpetuity of a high-level annual or regular periodic output of the various renewable resources of the national forests" (Coggins et al 1993, 622-623).

It is not difficult to see a connection between the U.S. policy of multiple uses with sustained yields and the idea of sustainable development defined by the

United Nations' World Commission on Environment and Development in 1987. As explained by R. J. Tobin, sustainable development "requires meeting the essential needs of the present generation for food, clothing, shelter, jobs, and health without 'compromising the ability of future generations to meet their own needs' " (Tobin 1994, 276). Both MUSY and sustainable development are founded upon a belief that human management of resources can continue to provide for the needs of growing populations without limit. Our faith in policies such as these must surely define the state of the art in environmental policy as we reach the close of the 20th Century, but they are not the only policies governing the national forests today.

In 1976, Congress passed the National Forest Management Act (NFMA), which mandates the recognition of interrelationships between biological and physical, therefore non-economic, factors in determining production targets for forest resources (Bowes & Krutilla 1989, 7). Also, and important to the purposes of this essay, NFMA requires the Forest Service to develop plans for each of its forests (Coggins et al 1993, 641). Planning under NFMA differs from previous planning methods in that local unit planning is no longer distinct from forestwide planning. It now requires use of the FORPLAN linear programming package in development of forestwide multiple-use plans (Bowes & Krutilla 1989, 35).

So begins the era of linear modeling in forest management, a technique that assumes output is proportional to input, the very assumption of the Newtonian calculus, from which the marginal analysis of modern economics is derived. We see that in its first 100 years, Forest Service policy has evolved incrementally -- merely applying the latest techniques to its fundamental mission of harvesting trees for the utilitarian purposes of the American people. True, its current approach is more sophisticated, requiring vastly more computing power than did the simpler techniques of Pinchot and his conservative philosophy, but the outcome is the same: greater marginal benefit from forest resources.

As it preceded NFMA by several years, the Endangered Species Act (ESA) of 1973 is apparently an exception to the "muddling through" of incremental policy making as applied to the national forests. ESA legally shelters species of flora and fauna listed as endangered or threatened from "virtually all human acts that could tend to diminish their stocks" (Coggins et al 1993, 784). It forces all federal agencies, including the Forest Service, to refrain from "any action that jeopardizes the continued existence of listed species or harms their critical habitat" (ibid.). Though it seems to be a true mutant of policy from a Forest Service perspective, when viewed from the U.S. Department of Interior's Fish and Wildlife Service, it is merely another step in the incremental protection of the nation's wildlife resource. President Theodore Roosevelt began the series when he declared the Pelican Island Bird Refuge Proclamation of 1903, and it has continued through several pieces of legislation important to the preservation of declining populations of certain species.

Because habitat is so critical to the success of ESA, scientists began thinking in terms of whole ecosystems, resulting in the *ecosystems management approach*. Ecosystems represent the whole of a set of biotic (living) and abiotic (non-living) components, as well as the energy processes between them, which have evolved together over a great deal of time and are now in equilibrium. The ecosystems management approach seeks to maintain or restore the overall health of entire ecosystems. It is holistic in scope. Unfortunately, ecosystems tend to be fairly sizable, and show little or no respect for the property lines of human beings, nor the functional boundaries of government agencies.

The ecosystems management approach has resulted in a great deal of discussion over the concept of "regulatory takings" by the government in implementing plans to protect critical habitat. Regulatory takings occur when government regulation lowers property values or interferes with private uses of property without taking possession of the property, as happens in "physical takings" (Coggins et al 1993, 229). An example is the case where a farmer is not allowed to drain and cultivate land found to be a wetland habitat critical to the success of migratory birds or an endangered species. The government has not taken title to the land, but it has prevented the farmer from sowing and reaping financial gain from the land, resulting in a taking of his property rights.

The ecosystems management approach also requires the involvement of a multiplicity of institutions within a given ecosystem. Government agencies exist solely to execute the acts of their respective legislative bodies. When Congress passes a law, it often specifies which agencies will execute the law. For example, while the Endangered Species Act potentially affects all federal agencies, it specifically requires the Fish and Wildlife Service to list species that are threatened or endangered. Thus, the Forest Service must now work with the Fish and Wildlife Service to ensure that it does not jeopardize the continued existence of listed species or harm their critical habitat through the management of its forest resources. Where the authority of the Forest Service was once sovereign within the boundaries of a National Forest, it now must work closely with the Fish and Wildlife Service, an agency that holds a significantly different view on how to manage that ecosystem.

Incrementalism is meeting with challenges from our observations of the real world. We turn now to more recent theories in which change does not occur smoothly along a continuous curve, but makes quantum shifts, punctuated equilibria, in the Forest Service as well as in the forest.

## ANTITHESIS

In the utilitarian tradition, the individual actor unknowingly enhances the welfare of the many when he seeks to enhance his own welfare. There are, however, innumerable cases in which we can see that actions taken for personal gain often result in personal gain for the individual at some cost to society. When such actions are aggregated they may result in class hierarchies in which classes seek to dominate one another with the hope of greater personal gain for the members of the dominant class.

Social ecology is largely concerned with the hierarchies found in society, and their effects on society and its constituents. It is based largely on the ideas put forward by Murray Bookchin, a social theorist, in his book, *The Ecology of Freedom*. Bookchin equates the hierarchies found in society with systematic domination of one group over another based on age, gender, ethnicity, wealth, knowledge, and any number of other factors that contribute to power in a society (des Jardins 1993, 243). Social ecology is especially applicable to undertakings in which we see the domination of one community by another. Because the utilitarian tradition promotes "the greatest good for the greatest number of people," larger communities can assert themselves based simply on the "greater good" they are seeking.

Communitarian ethics seeks to deal with the issues raised by social ecologists by framing a relational view of the individual as a member of the community, rather than a self-interested actor seeking only personal gain. For many communitarians, a "multiplicity of small and overlapping communities, cooperatively controlled by their members" is the solution to today's problems, in which a proliferation of large-scale, bureaucratic institutions, public and private, now serve our primary needs (Daly 1994, 139).

One notable writer of communitarian ethics is John Mohawk, who traces communitarian values back to the Great Law of Peace, a philosophy practiced by the Six Nations of the Iroquois Confederacy. In his view, the relationships of mutual respect and care that characterize a human community are extended to include all living creatures as well as the abiotic features that sustain them. In short, respect is extended to the earth itself, and Mohawk's message to the world "is a basic call to consciousness" (Daly 1994, 165). He then goes on to describe the form of government set up by the Six Nations. It is a government in which leaders are servants of the people, and everyone directly participates in the workings of government. He writes:

*Direct democracy, when it involves tens of thousands of people, is a very complex business, and there are many rules about how meetings are conducted, but the primary rule about the flow of power and authority is clearly that the power and authority of the people lies with the people and is transmitted by them through the "chiefs." The fact that all the people have direct participation in the decision of their government is the key factor for [ . . . ] success (Mohawk, cited in Daly 1994, 172).*

This description of the workings of government differs from that of the representative form found in the U.S. Here we elect representatives that set up and appoint multitudinous experts, technocrats, to deal with the problems of society, each concerned only with the single-dimensional aspects mandated by the legislation governing his or her government agency. Direct democracy, if allowed to work, could deal more effectively with the multidimensional problems of society by virtue of its own multidimensional makeup. But ethical analysis is not alone in beginning to consider the multidimensional aspects of the real world -- much of communitarian thinking is based on recent advances in multidimensional economic theories.

Some writers consider the ethics of economics as applied to the environment, and find the neoclassical economic paradigm lacking. These writers are not necessarily economists, but have come from other fields to affix blame for current environmental conditions on the false premises of the neoclassical economic paradigm.

In Garrett Hardin's highly influential essay, "The Tragedy of the Commons," we find a biologist eloquently arguing for human population control to prevent the destruction of the commons, Earth, in which we must live. He does so by challenging the utilitarian foundation upon which the neoclassical economic paradigm is based. Hardin asks the question, "can Bentham's goal of 'the greatest good for the greatest number' be realized?" He then offers two reasons why the utilitarian goal is impossible:

*The first is a theoretical one. It is not mathematically possible to maximize for two (or more) variables at the same time. [...] The second reason springs directly from biological facts. To live, any organism must have a source of energy (for example, food). This energy is utilized for two purposes: mere maintenance and work. If our goal is to maximize population it is obvious what we must do: We must make the work calories per person approach as close to zero as possible. [...] I think that everyone will grant, without argument or proof, that maximizing population does not maximize goods. Bentham's goal is impossible (Hardin, cited in Daly & Townsend 1993, 129).*

Hardin questions the basic tenets of marginal analysis, especially its inability to compare goods in making rational decisions because goods are incommensurable, and incommensurables cannot be compared. He leans on his biology background to tell the economist that:

*Theoretically this may be true; but in real life incommensurables are commensurable [emphasis is Hardin's]. Only a criterion of judgment and a system of weighting are needed. In nature the criterion is survival. [...] Natural selection commensurates the incommensurables. [...] Man must imitate this process (Hardin, cited in Daly & Townsend 1993, 130).*

To support the imitation of this process, economists must realize that they, too, are dealing with the criterion of survival -- for society as well as the individual. Currently, when finding the ratio of costs to benefits for a given policy alternative, economists must monetize all aspects of the policy, including the loss of benefits to future persons affected by the alternative. They do so on the assumption that the value of a dollar decreases over time. This is known as *discounting the future*, and is based on what economists call a "positive time preference" in which individuals prefer benefits now rather than later (Spash 1993, 118). The problem with this premise is that at some point the dollar goes to zero, which opens the door for abuses to future generations by the current generation. Spash writes:

*In fact, discounting the future at almost any positive rate creates insignificant present values for even catastrophic losses in the distant future. [...] In addition, because net costs are distributed across the future and net benefits received now, degrading the future environment is falsely attractive (Spash 1993, 119).*

This is a significant blow to the underlying assumptions of the neoclassical economic paradigm, but really only works at the margins of marginal analysis itself. For more fundamental questioning of the economics of the utilitarian tradition, we turn to Amitai Etzioni, a communitarian who has proposed a new economics he terms *socio-economics*.

Etzioni argues with the single-dimensional function of the utilitarian actor. He writes:

*Where the neoclassical assumption is that people seek to maximize one utility (whether it is pleasure, happiness, consumption, or merely a formal notion of a unitary goal), we assume that people pursue at least two irreducible "utilities," and have two sources of valuation: pleasure and morality (Etzioni 1988, 4).*

This *moral dimension* of the individual actor is based upon the communitarian ideal that individuals in a community do not choose their own good. Rather, "they find a common good as members of a distinct moral order" (Etzioni & Lawrence 1991, 62). At last we find the development of an economics that is prepared to deal not only with a single dimension -- utility -- but also with the multidimensional aspect of a moral grounding to our individual actions.

Roughly contemporaneously with the paradigm shift proposed by Etzioni, the field of environmental philosophy was greatly influenced by the work of Norwegian philosopher Arne Naess in 1973. Naess objected to what he termed the "shallow ecology" of efforts to reduce the singular environmental concerns of pollution and resource depletion. He proposed instead, *deep ecology*, a "relational, total-field" perspective of the environment that encourages humans to work within a holistic, nonanthropocentric framework in all that they do (des Jardins 1993, 215).

This relational perspective requires that we question deeply the assumptions underlying our every action -- at the individual level as well as at the level of public policy. Bill Devall and George Sessions would dub this questioning: *the work of cultivating ecological consciousness* (Devall & Sessions 1985, 8). This ecological consciousness stands "in sharp contrast with the dominant worldview of technocratic-industrial societies which regards humans as isolated and fundamentally separate from the rest of Nature, as superior to, and in charge of, the rest of creation" (65). J. R. des Jardins suggests that "[e]nvironmental challenges require not just new ethics, but a new metaphysics as well" (des Jardins 1993, 223). To which Devall & Sessions are eager to offer their core definition of deep ecology:

*Deep ecology goes beyond a limited piecemeal shallow approach to environmental problems and attempts to articulate a comprehensive religious and philosophical worldview (Devall & Sessions 1985, 65).*

This worldview looks to the traditions of Native American culture for inspiration, also to Eastern traditions such as Taoism and Buddhism. It finds resonance in the work of certain American writers: Thomas Jefferson, Henry Thoreau, and Ursula K. LeGuin to name a few (18). As an example of the power of deep ecology to be found in these traditions and writings, consider this excerpt from the *Tao Teh Ching* by Lao Tzu, ancient founder of Taoism as we know it today, here translated by J. C. H. Wu:

*The highest form of goodness is like water.*
*Water knows how to benefit all things without striving with them.*
*It stays in places loathed by all men.*
*Therefore, it comes near the Tao.*
*In choosing your dwelling, know how to keep to the ground.*
*In cultivating your mind, know how to dive in the hidden deeps.*
*In dealing with others, know how to be gentle and kind.*
*In speaking, know how to keep your words.*
*In governing, know how to maintain order.*
*In transacting business, know how to be efficient.*
*In making a move, know how to choose the right moment.*
*If you do not strive with others,*
*You will be free from blame.*
Lao Tzu (Wu 1961, 10)

Notice how Lao Tzu so simply, so subtly summarizes all of the work in this Antithesis. From social ecology to communitarianism to socio-economics, and now specifically to deep ecology, this tiny work gives us an approach that embodies "not just new ethics, but a new metaphysics as well."

These recent "advances" in the ways in which we look at the world in which we find ourselves and choose to act are not simply the latest examples of gradual social change, new theories based on the incremental evolution of the theories that preceded them. They are, in fact, examples of *punctuated equilibrium* in social theory. It is not because they are significantly different from their predecessors, or even because they suddenly arose out of the long stasis of utilitarian tradition and the neoclassical economic paradigm that they may be called examples of punctuated equilibrium. Communitarianism and deep ecology are not content to observe the actions of humans within their environment; they instead observe the actor observing itself acting. They conduct meta-analysis where neoclassical economics and its shallow environmental policy are content to conduct only analysis. This is the new criterion for survival. S. J. Goerner stated it well when she wrote:

*Forms which change forms (metaforms?) are thus most prone to survive because they can accelerate themselves. [...] They are forms that change themselves by learning not by physical change (Goerner 1994, 211).*

## SYNTHESIS

There are two dimensions along which evolution in forest management policy must occur: the ecosystem dimension and the social dimension. After discussing various aspects of how these dimensions are affected by the realities and possibilities mentioned above, a potential method for bringing the two dimensions together in a Forest Board will be prescribed.

Ecosystem dimensions, for purposes of this essay, include nonanthropocentric qualities of the forest as well as anthropocentric uses. First, there are meta-qualities describing characteristics of the ecosystem as a whole, specifically old-growth and biodiversity. These characteristics are defined in light of recent studies on their contribution to the well-being of the ecosystem itself. Next, there are natural resources produced and contained within the forest that make it invaluable from the perspective of anthropocentric uses. The five traditional resources named in the Multiple-Use, Sustained-Yield Act -- timber, range, wildlife, watershed, and recreation -- will be discussed from the perspective of an ecosystems management approach.

Old growth is an aspect of the temperate forest ecosystem that has various meanings to various points of view. To the ecologist, it may represent the climax stage of forest succession as characterized by F. E. Clements, in which the forest has not met with a major disturbance -- logging, fire, climatic change -- for hundreds, even thousands of years. As noted by D. Worster, "In some unique sense, [the old-growth forest] had become a live, coherent thing, not a mere collection of atomistic individuals, and exercised some control over the non-living world around it, as organisms do" (Worster 1993, 159). In short, the forest has taken on a life of its own, a maturity that allows the forest to manage its own energy flow unimpaired by external influences.

The tremendous energy held within old-growth forest attracts the attention of the human species as well. New Age environmentalists come to feel -- literally *feel* -- the energy of the forest, while loggers come to reap the harvest of old-growth timber, "highly valued because it is contained in large trees that produce high-quality, defect-free wood" (Booth 1992, 45). Unfortunately, these points of view do not enjoy the forest in easy harmony. The economic gains to be had from harvesting the product of centuries of uninterrupted photosynthesis, and the secondary gains to be had from managed second-growth stands, are of little use to the recreational user of the forest, whose enjoyment may be severely curtailed by vast stretches of clear cut. Even the distant sound of chainsaws ripping the solitude of the old-growth forest and the rumble of heavy equipment, even the easy access provided by logging roads may be detrimental to many recreational uses of the forest. But to the old-growth forest, they, the loggers and environmentalists alike, are both inimical to its well-being and the energy flow it has so arduously crafted, even evolved, and maintained for eons.

Simultaneously, old-growth directly influences that other meta-quality so highly valued by today's ecologists and recreational users: biodiversity. The very definition of old-growth, in which there is a climax species and its particular set of co-evolutionary, mutually dependent, dominant organisms, limits the diversity potential in the forest. In fact, a common means of measuring diversity, *Simpson's index of diversity*, which estimates the number of times we would have to take pairs of individuals at random to find a pair of the same species, is simply the inverse of one of ecology's most common measures of dominance in a community, *Simpson's index of dominance,* the total number of individuals in a species divided the total number of individuals of all species (Smith 1992, 301-304).

Biodiversity is essentially a measurement of the number of species coexisting within a biological community. Its definition is, however, under reconsideration in that ecologists now tend to put down their binoculars when looking for species richness, and pick up a microscope instead. Recent DNA analysis of the bacteria in a teaspoonful of Norwegian soil revealed not the dozen or two species that scientists expected, but two to ten thousand species (Snape 1996, 29). Not individuals -- species! Indeed, we are redefining our notions of biodiversity. W. J. Snape comments that "[w]e need a hierarchical set of indicators with monitoring and management tiered to one another and coordinated across different spatial scales [as scientists] increasingly realize how intricately ecological conditions and species interact" (ibid.).

Fortunately, science and forest management are finding common ground in theories and techniques based on chaos and self-organization. Chaos theory, the study of complex nonlinear systems so dynamic as to appear chaotic, has allowed us to adopt "new images and a new language to explain everyday organizational and policy phenomena" (Overman 1996, 77-78). We are fast applying this new language to policy decisions, even where they concern the chaotic, self-organizing characteristics of the forest. E. S. Overman writes:

*Chaos theory adds to our understanding of [...] behaviors. It fosters an appreciation, not distrust, of chaos and times of uncertainty and stress[.] While most managers and management methods attempt to seek some equilibrium through various control processes, and apply them even more tightly when order is dissipating, real change and new structures are found in the very chaos they try to prevent. There is also a certain faith in self-organization, not complacency but knowing that small actions can redouble many times over to create large effects -- or what chaos theorists call the butterfly effect (Overman 1996, 81-82).*

In the management of forest ecosystems, these ideas can be placed on the ground as islands and corridors, and their resulting ecotones. As R. L. Smith points out in discussing islands, or habitat fragments, "[a]s the size of an area increases, species richness also increases, up to some maximum point" (Smith 1992, 312). A longstanding rule of thumb was suggested by P. Darlington: *A tenfold increase in area leads to a doubling of the number of species (ibid.).* A number of studies have concluded that there are species that thrive only along the edges of forest ecosystems, also species that thrive only in the interior of undisturbed tracts of forest. The edge, or ecotone, of an ecosystem is where chaos and self-organization are played out so conspicuously. E. P. Odum defined the ecotone as "a transition between two or more diverse communities" (Odum 1971, cited in Holland et al 1991, 1), areas rife with potential for the bifurcations of chaos theory, those "moments of *choice* [emphasis is Overman's] in a system's evolution" (Overman 1996, 78). As the interior of the forest tract steadily organizes itself into some type of old-growth system, with its dominant species and selfish energy conservation techniques, biodiversity can be maintained, even increased, through the management of ecotones where chaos encourages a greater number of participants than in the more tightly bound ordered-complexity of the old-growth interior.

Thus islands and edges both have their place in the forest, and their proper management is essential to healthy forest ecosystems. Of possibly greater importance to the continued survival of many species is a blending of islands and edges known as corridors. Small-scale corridors may be as simple as culverts under roadways to allow animals safe access to habitats bisected or isolated by the road (Smith 1992, 318). On a larger scale, corridors may themselves be elongated tracts of old-growth that connect two or more fragments of old-growth forest. They may be based on the needs of specific migratory animals, or they may be constructed for migrations due to the climatic changes predicted by global warming. Whatever their design and intent, corridors certainly increase the amount of edge surrounding an ecosystem.

Forest management policy must therefore balance the goods of old-growth, biodiversity, and resource allocation. It must be done with great care and a great deal of knowledge at every site in which policy makers seek to manage the forest.

Of the forest resources, perhaps none is so highly valued in economic terms as that of timber. The harvesting of timber is also the most controversial of forest management policies. This is where the tension between economics and ethics, preservation and conservation, man and the environment is so evident. The problem is this: the harvesting of timber requires significant levels of labor and capital outlay in terms of loggers, equipment, and infrastructure. Profitable harvesting of timber demands a positive balance between revenues and expenses. The more wood harvested at a given level of expenses in labor, equipment, road-building activities, et cetera, the more profitable the venture will be. This neoclassical economic reality encourages the use of harvesting techniques destructive of large tracts of old-growth forest that are easily reached by road and waterway. And somehow, the Forest Service has been hoodwinked into believing it should increase the profitability of timber harvesting by offering its resources at levels that are far below fair market value.

The most inflammatory of harvesting techniques is that of clearcutting, "one of three variants of 'even-aged management,' a system aiming at a new forest in which all of the trees in a given area will be of roughly the same age" (Coggins et al 1993, 632). Clearcutting, as the name implies, means the complete removal of timber from a wooded area. It is not hard to see how, once logging equipment has been purchased, the road has been built, and the loggers have been hired, one would want to harvest every tree possible without the additional expense of more equipment, more infrastructure, or more labor.

There are variants of clearcutting less destructive to certain species, however, particularly the shade-intolerant and economically valuable Douglas fir (633). In the *seed tree method*, a few large trees per acre are left standing to provide natural propagation of the even-aged stand so important to the conservation techniques of Gifford Pinchot and his followers. Less destructive to other species is the *shade tree method*, in which more trees are left standing per acre on the premise that young trees of shade-tolerant species require some protection from direct sunlight. All variants of clearcutting eventually result in even-aged stands as the mature trees that had been left standing are soon removed in a second harvest that leaves little variation in the overall age of the resulting managed forest (632).

It is easy to condemn such practices as harmful to the forest ecosystem, but there may be healthful aspects if conducted properly. First, a great deal of edge is created while clearcutting and managing an even-aged stand, increasing the potential for biodiversity. Second, and perhaps more importantly, it may be less destructive from the perspective of the total ecosystem to allow the clearcutting of a relatively smaller portion of forest, with the corresponding decreased level of infrastructure required to harvest the same amount of timber.

An alternative to the even-aged management approach to timber harvesting is found in *selective cutting*, in which specific trees are culled in order to produce a more diversified forest (633). But are we really not just talking about a matter of scale? To the felled tree, there is absolutely no difference between clearcutting and selective cutting -- both are equally fatal. And to the myriad of organisms dependent on that felled tree, there is equally little difference between the two methods. To the ecosystem, it may be that there is a threshold of timber removal, beyond which the ecosystem is threatened, no matter whether the harvest was conducted intensively in a subsection of the ecosystem or selectively across the ecosystem as a whole. The amount of edge created in selective harvesting may be far less while the removal of old-growth is the same. And the requirement of more roads and a greater proportion of disturbed area, even if it is less disturbed, may actually be more detrimental than a restricted clearcutting. These are problems that must be considered on a site-specific basis, with a great deal of knowledge supporting the final decision. For, at least in human terms, the decision is final.

The range resource is another product of the forest specifically mentioned in the Multiple-Use, Sustained-Yield Act. Some 12,000 ranchers and farmers are permitted to graze four million "animal unit months" (AUMs) on approximately 100 million acres of National Forestlands (688). As suggested by these figures, the forage harvest to be had in our forests is not great, requiring 25 acres to support one cow for one month. Edward Abbey was typically acrimonious in his treatment of grazing on forestlands, as seen in this excerpt quoted by Coggins et al:

*According to most government reports (Bureau of Land Management, Forest Service), only about 2 percent of our beef, our red meat, comes from the eleven Western states. [...] More than twice as many beef cattle are raised in the state of Georgia than in the sagebrush empire of Nevada. And for a very good reason: back east, you can support a cow on maybe half an acre. Out here, it takes anywhere from twenty-five to fifty acres. In the red rock country of Utah, the rule of thumb is one section -- a square mile -- per cow (690).*

This dearth of range resource productivity in the National Forest must be considered when managing forestlands. Especially when one considers the increased erosion, diminished water quality, and diminished recreational enjoyment caused by grazing on forestlands, even wilderness areas. When one considers the additional destructive actions of fencing, predator control, and motorized roundups, along with loss of revenues due to grazing fees that are far below fair market value, the range resource is one that just does not make much sense for the forest manager. Unfortunately the range resource has powerful constituents, and the cowboy myth is ingrained in the American psyche as part of our western heritage, whether it helps us to meet today's problems or not.

The watershed resource has been dubbed the "forgotten multiple use" though it is "an important if not overriding priority in federal land management" (420). No good definition exists for what constitutes a watershed, other than the obvious geographical description of any area drained by a moving body of water. Yet there is the vague sensation that the quality of the watershed is an indicator of the health of the ecosystem that contains it. The problem arises in that watershed management generally means increased water yield for some downstream municipality, and the forest management method for increased water yield generally means felled trees. A healthy ecosystem retains water just as it conserves its own energy flow. If forest management has increased the water yield by removing vegetation, it has also likely damaged the ecosystem's ability to retain other goods.

The wildlife resource is another that is not easily managed simultaneously with intensive production of forest resources. Intensive timbering activities, especially clearcutting and its resultant even-aged stands, are obviously counterproductive to wildlife that require old-growth forest. Intensive grazing limits forage harvesting for non-domestic herbivores and disrupts the relationship between those animals and their predators, especially when the predators are exterminated by managers of the range resource. Intensive recreational use of the forest does not mix easily with the wildlife resource in that too many humans, even those with the best intentions, will spoil a habitat for wildlife. If they use motorized vehicles as part of the recreation experience, they endanger the well-being of wildlife even more. And the Endangered Species Act, based as it is upon single-dimensional goods, can be detrimental to the forest as a whole. W. J. Snape writes:

*Attempting to manage lands for one or a few favored species is more than inappropriate. In several circumstances, it can also produce pernicious effects. [...] Such restricted approaches to conserving "wildlife" or boosting quite local ("alpha") diversity have led us to chop up many managed landscapes into small fragments of habitat with abundant edge. Perversely, such management prescriptions applied across a landscape have had the effect of directly and dramatically reducing overall ("gamma") diversity (Snape 1996, 22).*

Finally, the recreation resource is often at odds with forest management intent on maintaining ecosystem health. Indeed, the recreation resource threatens itself! While motorized vehicles have greatly increased the ability of millions to reach and enter the National Forests, their presence within the ecosystem, including the pollution they create, the noise they generate, and their requirement for well-maintained roads and parking areas, has also greatly diminished the forest as a place of natural beauty untrammeled by humankind. And when recreation brushes up too closely against other forest activities such as logging, the recreation experience can be severely diminished.

Other social dimensions of forest management are no less difficult to maximize. Decreased reliance on the duality humans have constructed, setting themselves apart from the environment in which they find themselves, would seem to be a natural consequence of increased attention paid to forest management. But humans are deftly able to impose their notion of separation upon the forest, as evidenced by ideas like even-aged management, sustainable development, and the Endangered Species Act, in which single-dimensional human values of profit, quality of life, and favoritism that borders on speciesism, are maximized at the expense of a oneness with nature.

Diversity is as important among managers of the forest as it is in the forests that they manage. As noted by R. C. Paehlke, "Important points of value intersection -- sometimes conflictual, sometimes mutually supportive -- exist as regards gender and environment, class and environment, race and environment, and regional equity and environment" (Paehlke 1994, 363). Where the Forest Service has traditionally been predominantly white, middle-class, and male, there is a great deal of potential good to be had in utilizing the environmental values of women and members of ethnic minority groups. This is especially true when those "minorities" are in fact the local majority, as is often the case in and around National Forests of the Pacific Northwest. Paehlke points out, "parallels between the domination of women and the domination of nature" even to the extreme of parallels "so strong they reach into the very structure of our language as in the 'rape' of the land, 'virgin' forests, and 'mother' Earth" (ibid.).

The tendency of men to dominate their environment may be offset by the recruitment of more women into positions responsible for forest management. Likewise, an increased awareness of the values of minorities whose lives are intimately interwoven with that of the forest ecosystem may well signal the end of western separatist philosophy while it simultaneously better manages the multidimensional qualities of the forest itself. In assessing the prospects for integrating equity and environmental values, Paehlke concludes:

*Multidimensionality is accentuated and accelerated. Not that politics was ever simple. But ideology can no longer be seen in simplistic left-right/liberal-conservative terms (Paehlke 1994, 366).*

Finally, there is the intergenerational argument for preserving, restoring, maintaining, even creating goods available through forest management along both the ecosystem dimension and the social dimension. Former U.S. Senator Gary Hart argues for a new ideal in which *quality* is celebrated over the current lust for *quantity*. He defines it this way:

*The ideal of quality is based upon relationship -- each of us with our neighbors (the human community), all of us with nature (the community of nature), and each of us with our children (the future community). The central organizing principle of this new ideal must be to create and preserve the highest quality culture as our children's patrimony. From this, all economic and social policies should flow. The guiding principle is sufficiency rather than excess (Hart 1996, 183).*

To bring about the changes along the social dimensions discussed here, our institutions must change dramatically. We must invoke the strengths of metaforms -- forms that change themselves by learning -- to give us the creative, multidimensional solutions required by the rising tide of multidimensional problems facing managers of the forest today. Bellah et al, speak directly to the challenge before our institutions when they write:

*For all these reasons we need an extended period of serious and sustained national discussion: first, to learn why our ideology of Lockean individualism is inadequate for our new level of interdependence; and then to discuss alternatives that will safeguard our traditional concern for liberty and also more effectively conceptualize issues of the common good (Bellah et al 1991, 114).*

This statement is as relevant to the discussion of forest management as it is to any discussion of institutions in western society today. In the spirit of Bellah, a recommendation for an institution designed for the punctuated evolution of just such a discussion in forest management can now be made.

# THE FOREST BOARD

An evolutionary experiment in managing forestlands in the Pacific Northwest should be immediately undertaken. Call it the Forest Board. It is a self-organizing body of individuals, each of whom represents some aspect of the forest and the resources that it holds. Each Forest Board is responsible for one forest, that is, one ecosystem, under the care of the U.S. Forest Service. It is anarchic in that neither its goals nor the means for achieving those goals are clear. It is made up of as many people as are required to represent the interests of the forest -- some are appointed to the board, some are elected.

There are experts from various federal agencies -- representatives of each Act that applies directly to that forest. Obviously the Forest Service has one representative on the Forest Board. If there are species present, even formerly present, that are listed as threatened or endangered under the Endangered Species Act, a representative of the U.S. Fish and Wildlife Service will be appointed. National Biological Survey has been terminated since the writing of this essay. State agencies may wish to appoint representatives as applicable. Various industries will appoint one representative each to voice their concerns for use of the timber, range, and recreation resources. Downstream municipalities with concern for the watershed will appoint a representative. Local communities in and around the forest will elect representatives to ensure the highest quality culture as it pertains to issues of the forest. Native American communities with ties to the forest will elect representatives to ensure their direct participation in the affairs of the forest. There are as many representatives as the Forest Board agrees it needs to ensure the health of the forest. And where it can be determined, the interests of the unborn will always be represented by a vote against doing anything that may harm the forest for future generations.

In 1996, the residents of Colorado passed a constitutional amendment, Amendment 16 -- State Trust Lands, which predicts the Forest Board. The amendment, which got 52 percent of the vote (Kowalski 1996), changes the mission and makeup of the board that governs use of Colorado's three million acres of public lands granted at statehood to support schools and other public institutions. Important to this discussion, the amendment "changes the Colorado State Board of Land Commissioners' current constitutional duty of maximizing revenue from state trust lands to managing the lands to produce reasonable and consistent income over time" (Colorado General Assembly 1996, 34). The amendment also changes the organization of the board by "increasing the number of members on the board from three to five, requiring that specific areas of expertise be represented on the board, reducing the length of appointed terms from six to four years, limiting members' service to two consecutive terms, and eliminating the salary for board members" (Colorado General Assembly 1996, 34-35).

There are some good ideas here. And the electorate adopted them! Even if Colorado is only incrementally advancing its philosophy in managing state trust lands, these ideas may be incorporated into the punctuated evolution proposed for the Forest Board. For example, the trend toward larger boards is noted as important. Terms of Board members, whether appointed or elected, should be short and limited to ensure fresh ideas and a greater degree of participation. Service on the Forest Board should be voluntary in that citizen participants are not paid and government representatives do not receive pay beyond their regular salaries.

Yet while the Board members themselves are unpaid, all expenses incurred by the Forest Board, including the salaries of government representatives appointed to the Board, must be paid by the Forest Board out of its operating budget. And there should be some stipulation that a portion of all proceeds from the sale of forest resources -- timber, range, recreation, et cetera -- be paid to the federal government as royalties on resources owned by the People, for the People.

Thus, the Forest Board must generate revenues to offset the expenses it incurs through its own existence, and all revenues are generated from sale of forest resources. Beyond that, however, the Forest Board may elect to intensively produce revenues or it may elect to tread lightly upon the ecosystem within its care. Chances are good the latter route will be taken as there is no immediate financial gain for many representatives; indeed, there is a great deal of loss at stake in the moral dimension. Those representatives with financial interests will likely be quieted by the realization that all costs must be covered by generated revenues. There are no externalities -- positive or negative -- all costs are internalized. Every mile of road that must be built to extract resources must be paid for by the sale of those resources. Every Environmental Impact Statement must be paid for by the proponent of extractive activity, and the Forest Board does not appear as a line item on the budget of any agency -- federal, state, or local -- it must be self-sufficient and self-sustaining. This attitude toward the externalities of forest management will not only give pause to those who would reap its harvests, it will also give them a great deal of incentive to sell their resources at prices that at least represent fair market value. If Commerce and Labor are represented, one can rest assured that every last job will be eked out of every unit of resource before it reaches the consumer. The export of raw timber to the Far East at prices well below market value will be short-lived.

Membership of the proposed Forest Board is clearly differentiated from that of other boards that make policy over federal natural resources. In the case of the district advisory boards that formulate grazing policy on federal lands, members are elected by ranchers in secret elections (Coggins et al 1993, 705). The ranchers and the board members they elect hold deep-rooted values regarding their right to graze federal lands, and there are no voices for multiple-use, let alone ecosystem health, elected to these boards. *Diversity must be the defining characteristic of the Forest Board.*

In order to deal with the conflicts sure to arise from intentionally setting proponents of widely diverse forest activities on the Forest Board, the members may consider using a specialist in conflict resolution to assist them in the decision making process, keeping the members focused on the larger issue. Brewer & deLeon here emphasize the importance of the comprehensive perspective:

*Contextuality means understanding the relationship between the part and whole of a problem. It also means having a clear sense and appreciation of the past, present, and future of events as they interact and change through time. If a choice must be made, we urge comprehensiveness by giving preference to the whole (Brewer & deLeon 1983, 13).*

The vision statement of the Forest Board may be based upon lines from Aldo Leopold's "Foreword" to *A Sand County Almanac*:

*That land is a community is the basic concept of ecology, but that land is to be loved and respected is an extension of ethics. That land yields a cultural harvest is a fact long known, but latterly often forgotten (Leopold 1949, viii-ix).*

Similarly, the mission statement of the Forest Board may be based on Leopold's famous maxim from "*The Land Ethic*:"

*A thing is right when it tends to preserve the integrity, stability, and beauty of the biotic community. It is wrong when it tends otherwise (Leopold 1949, 224-225).*

## CONCLUSION

The capacity for an instance of punctuated equilibrium in forest management policy has been attained. We have gained sufficient knowledge of ecosystem behavior, ethical behavior, economic behavior, and institutional behavior for the *sudden* occurrence of metaforms capable of monitoring and regulating their own motivations as well as the health and well-being of the temperate forest ecosystem. The Forest Board described above is an example of just such a metaform, a self-organizing institution that is fully conscious of itself as an instrument of goods along both the environmental and social dimensions -- an actor observing itself acting.

## DEEP POLICY

At the heart of this consciousness is *deep policy*, a relational, total-field image in which all policy, current as well as proposed, is questioned at the deepest levels humans are able. Deep policy goes to the very core of human motivations and traditions to better understand why we behave in the manner that we do, and works to formulate and implement improved policies based on that better understanding. Deep policy discerns no separation between humans, their policies, and the environment.

Deep policy is transformative -- it encourages periods of accelerated evolution through increased consciousness.

Deep policy is metaphysical -- it forces self-realization in the knowledge that we, the forest, even the planet, and our policies toward the forest and the planet are one.

*Deep policy is evolving.*

## CRITICAL THINKING DRILLS

1.   Discuss the application of tenets of economics, such as discounting the future, to environmental issues other than logging. How does our economic theory change the value we place on an environmental resource?

2.   Think back on an occasion in which you were in a National Forest. Were you aware of the multiple uses conducted within that forest? How was your own use affected by the use of others? Do you feel they coexisted well, or did some uses prevent the full enjoyment of other uses? How would you resolve this conflict?

3.   Critique the concept of *deep policy* as used in this essay. Is it a metaphor that could transform our attitude toward environmental policies and their affect on the planet?

## RESEARCH FOR THE ADVENTUROUS

Read Edward Abbey's essay titled "Polemic: Industrial Tourism and the National Parks" from his book, *Desert Solitaire*. Are Abbey's ideas workable in today's National Parks. Write a 600-word essay describing his ideas for eliminating automobile traffic in the Parks in light of recent policy changes made to ease congestion in Yosemite and Grand Canyon National Parks.

## REFERENCES

Bellah, R. N., Madsen, R., Sullivan, W. M., Swidler, A., and Tipton, S. M. 1991. *The Good Society*. New York: Random House.

Booth, D. E. 1992. The Economics and Ethics of Old-Growth Forests. *Environmental Ethics* 14:43-62.

Bowes, M. D., and Krutilla, J. V. 1989. *Multiple-Use Management: The Economics of Public Forestlands*. Washington, D.C.: Resources for the Future.

Brewer, G. D., and deLeon, P. 1983. *The Foundations of Policy Analysis*. Pacific Grove, CA: Brooks/Cole Publishing Co.

Coggins, G. C., Wilkinson, C. F., and Leshy, J. D. 1993. *Federal Public Land and Resources Law.* Westbury, NY: The Foundation Press, Inc.

Colorado General Assembly, Legislative Council. 1996. "An Analysis of 1996 Ballot Proposals." State of Colorado, USA.

Daly, H. E., and Townsend, K. N., eds. 1993. *Valuing the Earth: Economics, Ecology, Ethics.* Cambridge, MA: The MIT Press.

Daly, M., ed. 1994. *Communitarianism: A New Public Ethics.* Belmont, CA: Wadsworth Publishing Co.

des Jardins, J. R. 1993. *Environmental Ethics.* Belmont, CA: Wadsworth Publishing Co.

Devall, B., and Sessions, G. 1985. *Deep Ecology: Living as if Nature Mattered.* Salt Lake City, UT: Peregrine Smith Books.

Etzioni, A. 1988. *The Moral Dimension: Toward a New Economics.* New York: The Free Press.

Etzioni, A., and Lawrence, P. R., eds. 1991. *Socio-Economics: Toward a New Synthesis.* Armonk, NY: M.E. Sharpe, Inc.

Goerner, S. J. 1994. The Physics of Evolution: From Chaos to Evolution and Deep Ecology. *World Futures: The Journal of General Evolution* 42:193-214.

Hart, G. 1996. *The Patriot: An Exhortation to Liberate America from the Barbarians.* New York: The Free Press.

Holland, M. M., Risser, P. G., and Naiman, R. J. 1991. *Ecotones: The Role of Landscape Boundaries in the Management and Restoration of Changing Environments.* New York: Chapman and Hall.

Kowalski, R. 1996. Trap ban, land protection win in end. *The Denver Post.* Nov 7, 1996. URL: http://www.denverpost.com/primary/new226.htm.

Overman, E. S. 1996. The New Science of Management: Chaos and Quantum Theory and Method. *Journal of Public Administration Research and Theory.* Vol. 6, 1, 75-89.

Paehlke, R. C. 1994. Environmental Values and Public Policy. Vig, N. J., and Kraft, M. E., eds. 1994. *Environmental Policy in the 1990s.* Washington, D.C.: Congressional Quarterly.

Smith, R. L. 1992. *Elements of Ecology.* New York: HarperCollins Publishers.

Snape, W. J., III. 1996. *Biodiversity and the Law.* Washington, D.C.: Island Press.

Spash, C. L. 1993. Economics, Ethics, and Long-Term Environmental Damages. *Environmental Ethics.* 15:117-132.

Tobin, R. J. 1994. Environment, Population, and Economic Development.

Vig, N. J., and Kraft, M. E., eds. 1994. *Environmental Policy in the 1990s.* Washington, D.C.: Congressional Quarterly.

Worster, D. 1993. *The Wealth of Nature: Environmental History and the Ecological Imagination.* New York: Oxford University Press.

Wu, J. C. H. 1961. *Lao Tzu: Tao Teh Ching.* Boston, MA: Shambhala Publications.

# INDEX

## R

range resource · 112
RAQC · 46, 47, 48, 51, 53, 55. *See*
    Regional Air Quality Council (RAQC)
Rawls, John · 96
    theory of justice · 96
    Two Principles of Justice · 96
recreation resource · 113
Regional Air Quality Council (RAQC) · 45
regulatory takings · 101
respiratory ailments · 34, 35, 36
risk · 15, 17
    independent causation · 16
    interdependent causation · 16
Rocky Mountains · 5, 9, 19

## S

self-sufficient · 19
Sierra Club · 79
SIP · 45, 46, 47, 48, 49, 50, 53, 55. *See*
    State Implementation Plan (SIP)
social dimension · 114, 115
social ecology · 20, 21, 102
social utility · 98
solar energy · 72
solar/hydrogen economy · 66, 68
solar-powered hydrogen production · 66
South Park · 9, 10, 11, 13, 14, 17, 18, 19,
    20, 21, 22, 23
South Park aquifer · 12, 13, 14, 17, 19, 21
South Park basin · 12
South Park Conjunctive Use Project · 10,
    12, 14, 15, 17, 18, 19, 21, 22, 23
South Park ecosystem · 23
South Platte River · 5, 9, 10
Spinney Mountain Reservoir · 10
standing · 75, 86. *See* standing to sue
standing to sue · **76**, 77, 78
    future generations · 84
    *Japan Whaling Association v.*
        *American Cetacean Society* · 81

*Lujan v. Defenders of Wildlife (Lujan*
    *II)* · 82
*Lujan v. National Wildlife Federation*
    *(Lujan I)* · 82
*Oposa v. Factoran* · 84
*United States v. SCRAP* · 80
State Implementation Plan (SIP) · 40
Stone, Christopher · 77, 79
    "Should Trees Have Standing?" · 79
street sanding · 48, 49, 51, 53
sulfur dioxide ($SO_2$) · 46
sustainable agriculture · 30
sustainable development · 17, 27

## T

Tarryall Creek · 9, 13, 14
The Wind · 63, 64
tiered fuel excise · 58
    carbon excise · 58, 59
    revenue neutral · 59
    road use charge · 58
    sulfur excise · 58
timber · 110
    clearcutting · 111
    selective cutting · 111
*Too Late* · 71, 73

## U

U.S. Department of Agriculture (USDA) ·
    99
U.S. Department of Interior (DOI) · 100
U.S. Fish and Wildlife Service (FWS) · 101
U.S. Forest Service (USFS) · 99, 114
    mission · 99
United States Constitution · 84
utilitarian · 15, 16, 97, 103
    utilitarian tradition · 14, 21, 96, 102,
        107
    utilitarianism · **14**